I0492342

Profit the Coming Market Crash

Tony Pow

Highlights

My motivation to write this book

I would like to share my experiences, both good and bad. I use simple-to-follow techniques using the free (or low-cost) resources available to us. I have been successful in investing for decades. I am enjoying a comfortable financial life. I do not hold back my 'secrets' as my children are not interested in investing. I offer you a small legacy in sharing my investing ideas.

If you are looking at how to make a 100% return overnight, there are many other books claiming to do so, and then this book is not for you. This book describes how to be a 'turtle' investor making a fortune gradually and surely. Before you begin, first define your objectives.

My steps to trade stocks (ETFs are far simpler)

1. Search for valued stocks (there are many strategies to choose from).
2. Evaluate the screened stocks by
   a. Fundamental Analysis.
   b. Intangible Analysis.
   c. Qualitative Analysis.
   d. Technical Analysis.
3. Sell stocks.
   Every 6 months (shorter duration for some strategies), perform the same as in Step #2 to determine whether you need to sell the stocks you own, or just keep them for another 6 months.

The power of market timing

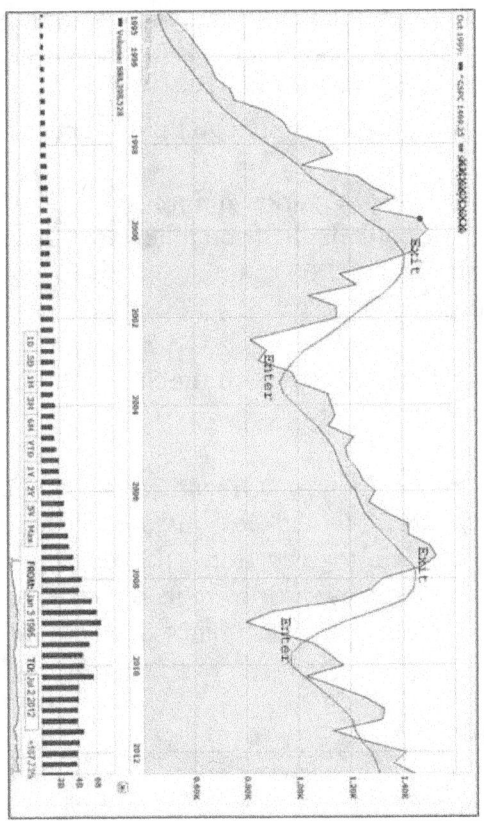

Most e-book readers allow you to select the graph to make it fit entirely on your screen. I use SPY, an ETF simulating the market. Detecting market plunges as seen in this graph indicates the exit points and reentry points also from 2000 to 9-2009 as follows.

Market Plunge	Peak	Bottom	Indicator Exit	Indicator Reenter
2000	08/28/00	09/20/02	10/01/00	06/01/03
2007	10/12/07	03/06/09	02/01/08	09/01/09
			08/01/11	11/01/11

Table: Vital Dates

For simplicity I skipped a few brief exits and reentries since 2011. You can run the simple chart once a month. When it indicates a potential market plunge is close, run the chart once a week. The last row represents a false signal.

This is based on stock prices so it may not identify the peaks and bottoms precisely, but so far it has not failed to avoid big losses and ensure big gains by reentering the market. I hope the next market plunge will most likely give us enough time to act as these two did.

Unbelievable return with market timing
Calculate how much you made if you followed the above exit points and reenter points from 2000 to today. I bet you would have made a good fortune.

I compared the above returns with the SPY without market timing from 1-2000 to 9-2013.

There are many assumptions. Dividends and compounding are not considered. My return should be substantially better if I include buying contra ETFs during the exits and selling them during the reentries. I was shocked by the incredible return by using this simple market timing. Again, past performance does not guarantee future performances.

Summary info:

S&P 500 1-2000 to 9-2013	With Market Timing	Without Market Timing
Better	**500%**	
Gain	1,000	167
Gain %	68%	11%
Annualized gained	5%	1%
Days	4,959	4,959

Calculations:

S & P 500	With Market Timing	Without Market Timing
1-2000	1,469[1]	1,469[1]
Exit 10/01/00	1,041[2]	1,041
Enter 06/01/03	1,041	964[4]
Exit 02/01/08	1,489[3]	1,379[4]
Enter 09/01/09	1489	1,020[5]
Exit 08/01/11	1,888	1,293
Enter 11/01/11	1,888	1,251
09/03/13	2,469	1.638
Gained	2,469 − 1,469=1,000	1,638-1,469=167
Gain %	1000/1469 = 68%	167/1469 = 11%

Annualized gained	68% * 365/4959=5%	11%*365/4959=1%
Better	(1,000-167)/167 = 500%	

Portfolio with Market Timing:

[1] Both start with S&P 500 of 1,469 on 1-3-2000.

[2] 10/01/00

The market timing portfolio exits the market and remains the same value of 1,041 until 6/1/00.

[3] 02/01/08

The market timing portfolio exits the market and remains the same value of 1,489 until 9/1/09.

'1,489' is calculated as follows:

1,041 * (1 + Rate) = 1,041 * (1 + 1,379-964)/964) = 1,489

where the S&P 500 is 964 on 6/1/00 and 1,379 on 2/1/08.

The other calculations are based on the S&P 500 at 1,020 on 9/1/9, 1,293 on 8/1/11, 1,251 on 11/1/11 and 1,636 on 9/3/13.

Portfolio without Market Timing:

[1] Both starts with the S&P 500 of 1,469 on 1-3-2000. We could use the 9/3/13 the S&P 500 value, but it would not account for some compounded interest considerations.

[4] S&P 500 is 964 on 6/1/00 and 1,379 on 2/1/08.

[5] 02/01/08. The portfolio value is calculated to be 1,020 as follows:

1,379 * (1 + Rate) = 1,379 * (1 + (1020-1379)/1379) = 1,020

where S&P 500 is 1,379 on 2/1/08 and 1,020 on 9/1/09.

The other calculations are based on the S&P 500 at 1,293 on 8/1/11, 1,251 on 11/1/11 and 1,636 on 9/3/13.

I cannot believe the shocking return with market timing. I checked my calculations and there was nothing wrong that I could find. If you find something wrong, send your findings to me (pow_tony@yahoo.com).

Even if I made a mistake somehow and got 100% instead of 500%, it still doubles the return without market timing! Ask any fund manager what it means to his or her fund performance and his / her career.

My simple technique that does not use chart told us to **exit the market** on around March 20, 2022.

Why you want to read this book

This book should improve your financial health substantially in the long run.

- A best seller with many editions written by a Ph.D. has all the convincing fundamental reasons why there will be a market crash with all kinds of bubbles going to burst. If you followed the book that was published in 2009, you are losing the potential profits from 2009 to today (2016). I bet you cannot time the market without technical analysis.

  The difference I can pinpoint good exit and reentry point is using technical indicators via charting, not just based on fundamentals. In this book I included another technique without charting.

- I had predicted there would be no crash in 2015 even the market was plunging in August, 2015. Why I was so sure? There was never been a down market in a year before the election year since WW2.

- This book could save you a lot of money especially if the 2017 market crash is correctly predicted. I have the reasons why it will happen. It is written by someone who times the market for the last 15 years, not by a salesman making a quick buck or by one with all the theories except an action plan.

- The chart has only one false signal and two correct signals from 2000 to 2010. Today we have more. However, false signals usually tell you to return to the market shortly.

- The recovery of oil price reduces the oil-producing countries to dump their securities. Watch the hike of the interest rate for 2017 especially if it is over 2% for the entire year.

- Even if it does not crash, it is a good insurance to stay a small portion in cash when the market is risky. The higher the market climbs, the deeper it will fall.

  A secular bull market requires no major war(s) as described in this book. Even in a secular bull market, we have market cycles within it.

- It shows you how to protect your investments for the coming market crash and future crashes. In addition, it also shows you when to re-enter the market and what type of stocks that have the highest appreciation potential.

- This book's chart has detected the last two market crashes correctly. It will work in the next market crash. However, it may not give us ample time to prepare or very close to the market peak like the last two.

  Even if you ignore the past performance, it is far profitable to use the simple, free chart to time the market than without.

  I also included how to detect market plunge without any chart. There are many other supporting hints based on my 15 years in REAL market timing. Most similar books just tell you the market is dangerous with no action plan.

  It has only 3 exit signals from 2000 to 2011: 2 good signals and one false signal. Since then, there are more false signals. False signals tell you to exit the market but shortly tell you to reenter the market. In most cases, there are no losses but tax consequences in the taxable accounts.

- There are books written by predictors on the market such as the Dow 40,000 and the popular 'coming' market crash book published around 2009 when the market started to recover. These books would cost you a fortune if you follow their advice.

  Some had decent predictions, but check how many right predictions they have since the right one. Usually none! It is usually their one-trick pony.

One best seller even asked you to exit in 2013 and even earlier in its initial edition missing all the profits from then to now (3-2015). I show you how and when to exit but not too early. I have only 15 years in actual market timing

- Besides market timing for the entire market, I also cover timing for sectors and stocks as a bonus to you.

- This book has about 170 pages (6*9) covering most topics in market timing. Hence, this book is forever, not just for 2017.

- I select proven ideas from more than 100 books besides my original ideas and experiences. I also include links to current articles that will bring more depth to the topic. It is not a novel or documenting the story of my life. All related chapters are grouped in a section for easy future reference. Some chapters are not easy to digest as they have a lot of pointers and some may require you to try them out yourself.

- You may ask why we invest. Our capitalistic system punishes us for not investing (i.e. taking risk). In the long run, stocks beat bank CDs by a wide margin. We just need to switch to cash when the market is risky and switch it back when it is not. It does not always work, but in the long run it does.

- This book is lengthy and requires you to try out the described techniques. The following chapters should give you the most bangs for your time: Chapter 5 and Chapter 4.

- Guided by the techniques described here, I have about 50% cash (my greed did not allow me to have more cash) before the August (2015) correction. I hope my previous readers have protected at least part of their investments.

- Check out my success stories.
  http://tonyp4idea.blogspot.com/2015/09/successes.html

- My articles in SeekingAlpha.com.
Click the link (http://seekingalpha.com/author/tony-pow/articles)

"Well written and keeps one's attention throughout the material Tony discusses. His thoughts to consider for 2017 are relevant and worthwhile. I have purchased the book and recommend others do as well. Success to all and thank you Tony." Bradley Hintze.

Contents

Bubbles

Bubbles have existed throughout our history. Bubbles occur due to the excessive valuation driven up by the big institutional investors (fund managers, pension managers, hedge fund manager, etc.).

Asset valuations are then driven even higher by the retail investors. As of 3/2014, the market bubble was caused by the government stimulus with the injection of capital into the excessive money supply and subsidies. The first investors riding the wave made good money and the last ones buying at the peak will the most.

From our recent history, we have the 2000 internet bubble, and then the 2007 (2008 for some) housing bubble. The chapter "Spotting Big Market Plunges" illustrates it was easy to detect the last two plunges. Read the chapter AGAIN and digest it. It could save you more than 25% of your portfolio in the next plunge.

Today all the mentioned bubbles could be caused by pumping too much money into the economy by the government. However, the government cannot keep on injecting money into the economy and then ask our children to pay our debts forever. When the injections stop, the market will drop fast and deep. As of 3/2014, the new Fed chairwoman most likely will not raise interest rates until the employment is lower than 6.5%. I estimate the interest rates will eventually rise and the market and the economy would most likely be affected adversely.

USD

As of 1/2014, the gold price has been down from its height of 1,850. It will most likely remain in the range between 1,200 and 1,900 until the USD appreciates to the next level and/or the global economies improve. The USD was doing quite well recently (actually at its highest level since 2008). It could be the other countries (EU and Japan) are doing worse than us, as Einstein said, "everything is relative". The strong USD is not good for exports and the global corporations would have less profit after converting back to USD. In addition, our shale energy is very promising, which will be clearer in two years whether it is just another mirage or not.

Bond

The bond bubble will burst when the interest rates rise. Also it will as the interest rates should have bottomed by now (2017). I do not believe it will go negative in the U.S. I prefer to buy contra ETFs against 20-year Treasury bonds (TBF). Besides bonds, farm products and the farm land have reached high price levels. The student loan could become bubble soon together with most other loans in many levels.

Stocks

There are several bubble stocks such as FAANGs, but they are few yet enough to move the entire market. From my technical indicators, the market is peaking and overbought as of 6/2014 (2019 in 20/20 hindsight). Play defense with stop loss orders. So far I am unable to find a potential trigger (a possible impeachment in 2019) if the interest rates remain low. However, the record margin debt is a big concern. When the credit is tightened (due to higher interest rates), this bubble will burst.

When to act

Unless you ask me nicely to borrow my time machine which is still under development, you cannot pinpoint when the bubble will burst. Your timing to act depends on your risk tolerance, your knowledge (a commodity trader can afford to take more risk on commodities for example), your greed, and your past experience could give you a false security.

Today, we have the housing bubble (2007-2008), the gold bubble, the market bubble (2015), the second housing bubble, the debt bubble (2015), the bond bubble, the second market bubble, etc. It seems like we can never get out of the bubble cycle. In 2019, the world would be in a global recession if the trade war between the two largest economies continue.

Since the world is economically connected better than before. When the U.S.A. sneezes, it affects our trading partners such as European countries along with China and Japan.

My incredible returns

Here are the three proofs for my incredible returns. Many of the techniques that I describe in this book in general terms.

Making 50% in one month

I claim to have the best one-month performance ever for recommending 8 or more stocks without using options and/or leverage. My following return was 57% in a month or 621%

annualized. They are slightly different as I calculated the average from the averages of three different accounts. The average buy date was 12/26/18 and the "current date" was after a month, 01/28/19 (Monday).

This performance may not be repeated. I will use the same screen for the coming years and even the expected 10% (or 120% annualized) is still very good.

I used the same screen for searching stock candidates and then evaluated the top searched stocks. I spent a total of about 20 hours from Dec. 15, 2018 to Jan. 5, 2019.

Stock	Buy Price	Sold Price or Current Price	Buy date	Sold Date or Current date	Profit %	Profit % annualized	Status
CHK	2.13	2.99	01/03/09	01/18/19	40%	982%	Sold
MNK	16.41	21.45	01/03/19	01/25/19	31%	510%	Sold
MNK	16.43	21.45	01/03/19	01/25/19	31%	507%	Sold
NNBR	5.68	8.58	12/26/18	01/28/19	51%	565%	
NNBR	5.72	8.58	12/26/18	01/28/19	66%	727%	
ESTE	4.35	6.45	12/26/18	01/18/19	48%	766%	Sold
LCI	4.61	8.29	12/21/18	01/28/19	80%	767%	
MDR	8.01	9.13	01/08/19	01/28/19	14%	255%	
YRCW	3.29	5.78	12/21/18	01/28/19	76%	727%	
YRCW	3.26	5.78	12/21/18	01/28/19	77%	742%	
ASRT	3.56	4.18	12/26/18	01/28/19	17%	193%	
UTCC	7.13	11.00	12/26/18	01/28/19	54%	600%	
YRCW	2.92	5.78	12/26/18	01/28/19	98%	1083%	

Best one-year return

I claim to have the best-performance article in Seeking Alpha, an investing site, for recommending 15 or more stocks in one year after the publishing date without using options or leverage. The link is:

https://seekingalpha.com/article/1095671-amazing-returns-velti-alcatel-lucent-alpha-natural-resources

You will find in the following link how I calculated the returns.

http://seekingalpha.com/article/2492255-a-tale-of-2-portfolios

My sector performance

As of 3/2019, the investment in my sector rotation account has returned about four times. The fund has been held for many years. It proves nothing about performance but sector rotation works for me. It is complicated to calculate the annualized returns as the funds were added two different times and I did not track those dates.

How to beat the S&P 500 index by 100%

I recommended 20 stocks in an article Amazing Return in Seeking Alpha, a website for investors. If you bought them on the published date and then you would have beaten the S&P 500 index by over 100% without considering dividends as demonstrated in my other article A Tale of Two Portfolios. One of the many techniques is my Pow P/E as illustrated in another article The Mysteries of P/E.

Let's say I made a mistake and it is only a 10% gain. How many fund managers can beat the S&P 500 index by 10% regularly?

Book I. Coming Market Crash

This book consists of three books: Coming Market Crash, Market Timing and Technical Analysis. The first book describes the expected crash and how to prepare it and the second book describes market timing in detail. This book will be updated to reflect my experiences in this period.

Introduction

Today the market is risky. That's why I write this book evaluating the possibility of a coming market crash. My simple technique that does not require charts told us to leave the market on around March 20, 2022.

It has been more than 10 years since the market recovered in 2009. It is overdue for a market plunge. We need about three market plunges to get back to our regular frequency ratio of about 2.5 in 10 years.

If you follow my market timing, we have experienced some false signals. However, a corrective signal tells you to reenter the market and hence most of the time you do not lose anything except the tax consequences in taxable accounts. Besides exiting the market briefly, you are still fully invested most of the time. It is far better than a best seller that tells us to exit the market even in 2009.

Conservative investors should sell their riskiest investments and accumulate some cash today. Market crash could have caused more than 40% loss from the peak. My market timing techniques will not detect the peak but would reduce further losses. In addition, cash is king during market crash as they can reenter the market with cash. That's how big fortunes are made. Imagine the big bargains in buying houses in 2008 but not the 'bargains' in internet stocks in 2000.

Previously we did not find any triggers. Today the trigger is the trade wars, particularly the one with China, the pandemic and the inflation.

This book explains why we may have a market crash coming and how to prepare it. It also includes simple techniques (no subscription and no tool to buy) to detect market plunges that have worked in the last two major market plunges. It will not identify the peaks and bottoms (and no one can). It may not give us ample time to prepare as the last two.

Our simple chart tells us to exit and reenter only two times from 2000 to 2010 and it has only one false alarm telling us to exit and return briefly (more false alarms from 2011 to 2016). The market before 2000 was quite different to today's market and that is why I did not use the older data. You should use this book as a reference and study market timing before you commit fully.

This book gives you tools to check the soundness of both fundamentals and technical indicators of the market. When both turn out to be unsound, to me it is the time to leave the market. We have two methods to determine the technical indicators of the market: one does not require charting and the other does.

We will face false signals to tell us to leave the market and then tell us to return. In most cases, the losses are inconsequential except for the taxes in non-retirement accounts.

In this risky market, I recommend using trailing stops for the appreciated stocks. In a nutshell and as an example, you place a stop loss of your appreciated stock based on the current stock price (vs the stock price you paid for). I prefer 10% below the current market price or lower depending on how volatile the stock is and your risk tolerance.

Links
Google or Facebook "Market crash 2020 (or the current year).
Here are some: Trade War, Barry, Recession

https://www.youtube.com/watch?v=kQftC4Vcl-s
https://www.youtube.com/watch?v=SqxXav1N5M0
https://www.youtube.com/watch?v=3eYyAiDhYkA

About the author

I graduated from Cal. State University at San Jose in Industrial Engineering and University of Mass. in Amherst with a MS in Industrial Engineering. My last job was in IT. I have been an investor for over 30 years.

Click the link for my articles in SeekingAlpha.com, a financial site.

Dedication

To all retail investors and future retail investors including my grandchildren. I sincerely hope this book will build bridges with fellow investors with different backgrounds.

Acknowledgement

Thanks to Seeking Alpha, Fidelity, Wikipedia and Investopedia for the many helpful links to enrich this book, and Yahoo!Finance and Finviz.com for the tools and charts used in this book.

Important notices

© 2018-2022 Tony Pow.
Emails to pow_tony@yahoo.com.

Version	Paperback	e-Book
1.0	01/18	01/18
2.0	11/19	11/19
2.4	05/22	05/22

No part of this book can be reproduced in any form without the written approval of the author.
Book store managers can order the paper version of this book from Createspace.com.
https://tonyp4idea.blogspot.com/2020/12/book-managers.html

Book update.
https://ebmyth.blogspot.com/2020/12/updates-for-all-books.html

Disclaimer

Do not gamble with money that you cannot afford to lose. Past performance is a guideline and is not necessarily indicative of future results. All information is believed to be accurate, but there is not a guarantee. All the strategies including charts to detect market plunges described have no guarantee that they will make money and they may lose money. Do not trade without doing due diligence and be warned that most data may be obsolete. All my articles and the associated data are for informational and illustration purposes only. I'm not a professional investment counselor, a tax professional or any other field. Seek one before you make any investment decisions. Remember to consult with a registered financial adviser before making any investment decisions. The above mentioned also applies for all other advice such as on accounting, taxes, health and any topic mentioned in this book. Tax laws change all the time, so talk to your tax advisors before taking any action. Some articles may offend some one or some organization unintentionally. If I did, I'm sorry about that. I am politically and religiously neutral. I have provided my best efforts to ensure the accuracy of my articles. Data also from different sources was believed to be accurate. However, there is no guarantee that they are accurate and suitable for the current market conditions and /or your individual situations. The values of some parameters such as RSI(14) are arbitrarily set by me. I have made a lot of predictions that may not materialize. My publisher and I are not liable for any damages in using this book or its contents.

How the rate of return is calculated

They are for education purposes only, and do not make your investing decisions based on them. I usually use annualized for better comparisons; 4% in a month is more than 5% in a year for example. For short-term strategies including momentum, shorting and year-end strategy, I use the returns for a month, and sometimes including returns for 2 months for comparison. Annualized returns are usually used for long-term strategies. The holding periods may have a few days off due to holidays and weekends. For simplicity, most of my returns do not include commissions, exchange fees, order spread and dividends. Most numbers have been rounded up for better readability. The return = profit / investment. I and my publisher are not liable for any error. I use SPY and sometimes RSP as a yardstick; RSP and SPY have the same S&P 500 stocks, but the stocks are weighted evenly in RSP. However, many readers do not know RSP.

1   Reasons for the coming market crash

This is an **example** for 2021 only. For the last few years, most market predictors have had their crystal balls broken. It is due to the excessive supply of money that leads to a non-correlation of the economy and the stock market. It cannot last forever. It will correlate again when the money supply is reduced.

The incredible recovery of the market from 2007-8 is due to the excessive printing of money (i.e. money supply). History is repeated again in 2020. It leads to easy credit to buy stock (margin debt) and buyouts/corporate profits. With more money to buy stocks and fewer stocks to buy (buyouts), it is a simple case of Supply and Demand.

Since World War II, we never had a down year in a year just before the election including 2007 and 2019. However, 2021 could be a tough year and the market bubble may finally burst. As usual, there are two camps arguing in opposite directions for predicting the market direction of 2021. I recommend my readers to take some actions, the same as buying insurance. As of 1/2021, the market is unsound fundamentally but sound technically. When the technical is unsound, it is the time to leave the market as indicated by the simple market timing illustrated in this book.

Consult your financial advisor before taking any actions, and I am not responsible for your gains or losses.

Good News

- We have hopes on the ending of this pandemic at least reducing the impact in 2021.
- The economy is improving slowly except in some sectors that are affected immensely by the pandemic.
- Energy cost could be bottom that is good for the energy sector. Judging by the forward P/Es of many energy companies, I do not believe green energy would take over in 2021.

- The interest rate is almost zero and that is good for the housing sector and related sectors, buybacks, margin interest rate and investing by the corporations.

Bad News

- It has been one of the longest bull markets.
- The economy is poor compared to one year ago with a high unemployment rate.
- Many small businesses such as restaurants will be closed forever.
- The record-high market is a bubble to many.
- Margin debt is at a record high.
- The government is running out of tools to revive the economy such as lowering interest rates. Excessive supply of money will hurt the economy in the longer term.
- The national debts (partly due to our endless wars) and obligations (partly due to our aging population) are high as a percentage of the GDP.
- Most foreign countries except Japan have been reducing buying our national debt. Most of the debts were purchased by the Fed by printing money excessively.
- Many retailers that cannot service their debts will go bankrupt if not already.
- The USD is weak and the status of a reserve currency is shaken. However, a weak USD is good for export, but not good for the profit for global companies.
- I expect higher inflation is coming.

Summary

2021 could be very risky. We're living dangerously on borrowed time. Hence, be conservative. The recent rise of the market is due to supply (excessive printing of money) and the demand (fixed number of assets). The market is not rational compared to the economy.

2   How to prepare for it

I like to repeat: No one can predict the market precisely and consistently unless s/he has a time machine. However, the more educated the guess, the better the chance to be materialized. The market may crash in 2021. Consult your financial advisor before taking any actions and I am **not responsible** for any loss or gain.

- Reduce buying stocks in my taxable account. It is harder to switch to cash if I consider taxes.

- Accumulate cash slowly during market cash. The money market in my broker's accounts pay nothing and the one in my annuity even charges a small fee. I switch most to CDs with different mature dates in case I need cash to buy contra ETFs.

- Will buy contra ETFs when market is plunging. It is for aggressive investors only.

- Buy value stocks which would lose less in a market plunge. However, cash and CDs are better in risky market. Avoid bubble stocks that have high P/Es.

- Avoid small cap stocks (less than 500 M for me). Large cap stocks lose less than small cap stocks in a market plunge as most investors believe small caps would be out-of-business.

- I would watch and act on the technical indicator SMA-350 of SPY. When the price dips below SMA-350, I will start selling most of my holdings. From 2000-2010, we have two correct signals to tell us to exit the market and one false signal, which tells us to exit the market but tells us to return to the market shortly. Since then, we have more false signals. Hence it is not perfect, but better than acting with some unproven strategy.

- Market plunges will be fast and steep. If the timing is correct, most stocks will be down. The following are the results of the last bear market. Contra ETFs have best performances. Shorting over-valued stocks could be very profitable but it would take time to evaluate them.

- RYTPX and GRZZX did very well in the last bear market (11-1-2007 to 2-28-2009). They are riskier with leverages.

Afterthoughts

Here is how a popular writer prepares: I and II.
http://seekingalpha.com/article/3105706-preparing-for-a-market-collapse
http://seekingalpha.com/article/3494496-preparing-for-a-market-collapse-part-ii

When to return to the market

The trillion-dollar question is: Is it a crash or a fierce correction?

Many factors on corrections are described in the book. However, corrections are harder to detect. A book is just a book. It is based on historical data (2 last market crashes for me) and every market is different.

For conservative investors, use 40% for this crash if it is one and 12% for corrections. Recommend use even lower numbers so you do not miss the boat but at the risk of coming back too early. If you feel the crash would last for a year, buy some CDs that mature in 1 year, which better than your broker's account collecting virtually no interest. Refer to **Disclaimer** in Introduction.

The following articles are about this sharp fall. Google "Market crash 2020).

Filler: The best complement

My late mother loved Wheel of Fortune. Why it is the best complement you may ask? She did not speak English.

3   Simplest market timing

Why market timing

Before 2000, market timing was a waste of time. However, after that, we have had two market plunges with the average loss of about 45%. It sounds harder to time the market than it actually is. We have a simple technique to detect market plunges and when to reenter the market. Our objective is reducing the loss to 25%.

Market timing depends on charts; the following describes how to use chart information without creating charts. Most charts will not identify the peaks and bottoms of the market as they depend on data (i.e., the stock prices). However, it would reduce further losses. It is simpler than it sounds. Just follow the procedure below.

The first part of this technique detects potential market plunges, and the second part advises you when to start reentering the market. It applies to individual stocks too. It also works to detect the trend of a sector (entering an ETF for the specific sector instead of SPY) and a specific stock.

Step-by-step procedure

When the market timer indicator (Death Cross) described next tells you to exit the market, sell SPY (an ETF simulating S&P 500). Do not forget to buy back SPY or similar ETF such as RSP, when the indicator (Golden Cross) tells you to return.

My experiences in 2000s

Basically I did the same as the above with some adaptations. I worked for a mutual fund company and they did not allow me to trade stocks effectively. However, I was allowed to trade sector funds offered by the company. Every two months, I switched to the sectors with the best performances for the last month. When most sectors were down for the last month, I rotated them to the money market fund. In March or April, 2000, I switched to traditional sectors from high-tech sectors (better to switch to market money funds). During that time, I bought stocks that had enough cash to last more than two years judging by their burn rates. The indicators should do a better job.

How to detect market plunges without charts (similar to <u>Death Cross</u>)

1.   Bring up Finviz.com.

2. Enter SPY (or any ETF that simulates the market) or RSP, equally-weighted SPY.
3. If SMA-200% is positive, it indicates that the market plunge has not been detected and you can skip the following steps.
4. The market is plunging if SMA-50% is more negative than SMA-200%. To illustrate this condition, SMA-200% is -2% and SMA-50% is -5%.
5. Another hint: B/S (buy sell ratio) is negative, specially it is more negative than last week.
6. Conservative investors should sell most stocks starting with the riskiest ones first such as the ones with negative earnings, high P/Es and/or high Debt/Equity. Obtain this info from Finviz.com by entering the symbol of the stock you own.
7. Aggressive investors should sell all stocks. Extremely aggressive investors should sell all stocks, buy contra ETFs such as PSQ, and even short stocks. I do not recommend beginners to be aggressive.

Example
As of 2/12/2022, the following are from Finviz.com.

ETF	SMA-200	SMA-50	SMA-20	Death Cross?
SPY	-0.8%	-4.2%	-1.7%	Yes (Step #4)
RSP	-0.5%	-1.9%	0.4%	Yes (Step #4)

Both ETFs indicate the market is a confirmed crash from my indications using a technique similar to Death Cross. However, they are quite close, and we should keep an eye on these numbers. In this case, SMA-20 has not been used. If it is a false alarm, the Golden Cross would indicate it and you should return to equity; it could be quite common in volatile markets. The futures indicate that on Monday (2/14/22) the market would plunge further. Another test is using SMA-350: When the current price is below SMA-300, it is a crash. SMA-20 has to be more negative than SMA-50 and it has not been used here.

Simple chart example. Bring up StockCharts.com and enter SPY. It indicates Death Cross occurred on around March 20, 2022.

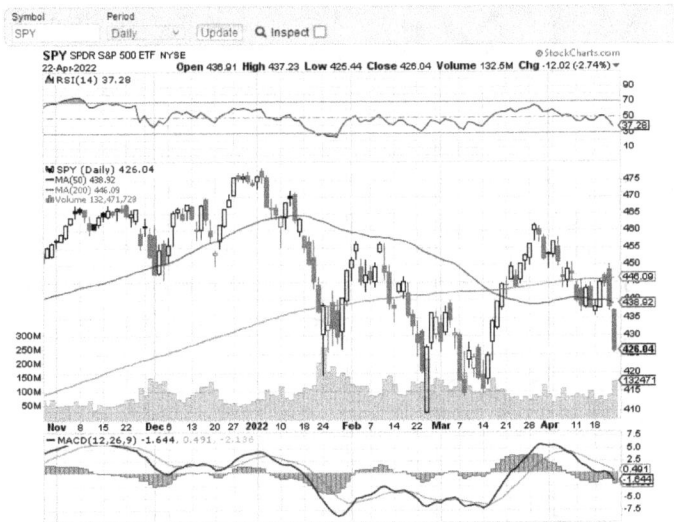

When to return to the market (similar to <u>Golden Cross</u>)

Use the above in a reversed sense to detect whether the market has been recovering. However, when the SMA-200% turns positive, I would start buying value stocks (low P/E but the 'E' has to be positive, and/or low Debt/Equity).

1. Bring up Finviz.com.
2. Enter SPY (or any ETF that simulates the market).
3. If SMA-200% is negative, the market is not recovering, and you can skip the following steps.
4. Sell all contra ETFs and close all shorts if you have any.
5. Market recovery is confirmed when SMA-50% is more positive than SMA-200%. To illustrate this condition, SMA-200% is 2% and SMA-50% is 5%. Commit a large percent of cash (or all cash for aggressive investors) to stocks. If you do not know what to buy, buy SPY or an ETF that simulates the market.
6. Another hint: B/S (buy sell ratio) is positive, specially it is more positive than last week.

How often should you check the market timing indicators?

Do the above once a month. When the SPY price is closer to SMA actions percentage, perform the above once a week. The charts and data for market timing described in this book are based on SMA-350 (Simple Moving Average) that is more preferable than this simple procedure, but it requires some simple charting.

Nothing is perfect

If the market timing is perfect, there would be no poor folks. The major 'defects' are:

- It does not detect the peak / bottom as it depends on past data. However, it would save you a lot during the crash.
- It is hard to determine whether it is a correction or a crash.
- From 2000 to 2010, there was only one false signal. The indicator tells you to exit and then tells you to reenter the market shortly. In most cases, you do not lose a lot. After 2010, we have more false signals.
- The market may not be rational or may be influenced due to specific conditions such as excessive printing of USD. If you do not mind charting, use SMA 350 (or 400) using SPY. Buy when the price is above SMA-350 (or SMA-400), and sell otherwise. SMA-400 reduces the number of false signals, but it is not nimble.
- I do not recommend Bitcoin but agree with most of thinking of this YouTube.
  https://www.youtube.com/watch?v=a5J8gMrEZxg

4   The economy

After Trump was elected, we have had a brief stock market rally. The market is usually ahead of the economy by about 6 months. However, they have been non-correlated since 2009. Let's examine the US economy briefly here.

Reduction of individual tax and corporate tax
The reduced corporate tax could stimulate the economy and it could lure some corporations to return their HQs to the US. The downside is that we need the revenues to finance the infrastructure projects.

China
We have been financed by the Chinese via selling our treasuries. China is switching their reserves to the "One Belt, One Road" projects.

Easy money is going away
CEOs should manage their corporations instead of boosting the stock prices via some easy financing.

Interest rates will be up
Investors should be careful about the hikes of the interest rates. As long as it is 1% or less for 2017, it should have little impact. To illustrate this, if the rate hike is 1%, you lose 10% interest on a 10-year bond. However, you only lose 2% if it is a 2-year bond. With our recent record-high of margin in buying stocks, the market could crash when interest rates surge.

Inflation
Historically it is about 3% and currently it is about 2%. If your CD returns 1% and inflation is 2%, you lose 1% but you need to pay taxes on the interest of a 2% CD. Uncle Sam is always the winner. When too much money is chasing a limited number of goods, we should have a higher inflation rate.

Bankruptcy & loan delinquencies
Corporations will bankrupt if they cannot pay back their loans, or are not able to pay their lawsuit claims. Personal bankruptcies increase if there are more small businesses that fail.

5 Articles on the current market

There are many such articles from Seeking Alpha, Market Watch, Yahoo!Finance, Google Finance... The following are some of them. There are always two camps: No crash and crash. Evaluate each of them and notice the date the article was written. Again, market plunge is the time to exit the market and market corrections provide opportunities to buy. I bet the coming one is market plunge.

Click the name of the article or for paperback readers enter the link to your browser. They are samples but not updated by the time you read this article Google current articles. Advisor Perspectives have some neat articles.

Argue that market is crashing

https://seekingalpha.com/article/4283057-inflation-recession-buy-energy-shares?v=1565282332&comments=show

Time to Sell
http://seekingalpha.com/article/4026143-now-might-right-time-sell-stocks-conservative-investors

Individual Investor Sentiment May Be Too Bullish
http://seekingalpha.com/article/4026188-individual-investor-sentiment-may-bullish

Playings fire: http://www.marketwatch.com/story/stock-market-bulls-are-playing-with-fire-says-financial-blogger-2017-06-21

Market Breath: http://www.marketwatch.com/story/beneath-the-glow-of-stock-market-records-darkly-bearish-trends-are-lurking-2017-08-04

More: 1 2 3 4 5 6 7

Argue that the market is not crashing
Riding The S&P 500 Wave
http://seekingalpha.com/article/4026367-riding-s-and-p-500-wave

6   Market long-term outlook

The market long-term outlook is not promising. Some of the following five factors may not be avoidable and I wish most of them will not happen in my life time.

1. Retirees are withdrawing their investments

It is not avoidable as the baby boomers (born after the WW2) have been retiring and the millennials with the college loans and a weak job market do not contribute enough to offset the withdrawals. This imbalance also affects every aspect of our economy such as the outpour of entitlements, housing...

2. Conflicts with China

We're having trade wars with China that would lead to a military war triggered by China's disputes on islets and the invasion (reunion depending on your view point) of Taiwan. I have written the article "Why a war with China?" However, the risk has been reduced recently. It is due to China's military advances that are enough to defend her coast line. US would not win without a lot of damages. The balance of power would lead to peace.

3. Endless wars

These wars drain our resources which should be spent in our failing infrastructures. Our next generation(s) will pay for our debts. The politicians want to buy votes from voters who want to receive maximum benefits with minimum contributions. Debts will continue to increase. Do not drive the mad dog (N. Korea) to a corner.

4. Loss of reserve currency status

With mounting debts, the USD has been weakened. It is good for our export and repaying our debts. However, it is bad for foreigners to invest in US. It happened to the market collapse for the Brits.

There are evidences that China is cutting down the Treasury bills – they are #1 or #2 foreign countries in owning our Treasury bills. The "One Belt, One Road" projects could cost over 1 trillion. Guess what currency they use? China still has a long way to achieve the status due to her inadequate regulations and experiences.

5. Natural disasters

There have been many recently. The major one could be the big earthquake in Pacific coast that has been long overdue.

The following topics are related.

A weakened US dollar

The impact of the weakness of USD:

1. More competitive to our export (good for US).
2. Less profit when foreign profits converted to USD (good).
3. Cheaper USD payments to our loans to foreigners (good).
4. Less attractive to invest by foreigners (bad).
5. Losing reserve currency status (really bad). I bet China is selling and cutting down buying our Treasury bills. They need to use the money for the "One Belt, One Road" projects. Most likely they will use Yuan to finance these projects.

Our huge trade deficit with China

It is about 400 billion a year in 2017. Are our products not competitive, or China has been setting up too many trade barriers? I believe both are true to some extent.

The figure is exaggerated a little. The raw materials are sent to China to assemble using lower-wage labor and sent them back to the US as finished products.

Using iPhone as an example, it is designed in US, assembled in China, using rare earth elements in China, using components from all over the world, and enjoyed by global consumers. The design cost should be deducted from the finished product when it is imported back to the US.

Our politicians suggest heavy tariffs on Chinese products. Most likely Chinese will fight back with same and it would lead to a trade war. Both sides will suffer. They will end and the politicians from both sides will declare victory. Seen this many times.

7   Falling oil price

When oil price is down below $30, I believe it is a buy to the investors. 3/2020 is the second chance after 1/2016. It may happen again in 2021. We had a chance to buy when the oil price fell almost to zero. The long-term future of oil is not that good. Many countries are switch to green energies. However, it is far less polluting than coal. In Dec. 2020, I found many oil companies had attractive forward P/Es.

The cost of the oil depends on the following factors:

- The ease of drilling. The production cost for most oil ranges from $2 to $20. Most drillers are not profitable when the oil price per barrel is below $50. Most cheap oils (close to the earth surface) have gone except in Saudi Arabia.
- The quality of oil. Most of Saudi Arabia's oil are good quality while Venezuela's oil is heavy and very expensive to refine.
- Transportation. It is least expensive if it is close to the customer. Venezuela has a long way to transport except the U.S.A.
- Competition of shale energy and now the reduced cost of green energy such as solar and wind.

High oil reserve (Venezuela is among one of them) does not mean high production due to the above factors.

#Fillers: I wish I have a time machine

After collecting bottles for money, an old lady ordered a bowl of plain rice and ate by herself. I wish I could have ordered a meat dish for her as I was 'ashamed' of being generous.

A well-dressed gentleman offered his just-bought hamburger to a beggar. The beggar refused and asked for money instead – most likely he needed the money to buy liquor. A tale of two citizens.

During a lunch with my fellow tourists, a beautiful girl danced for our entertainment. I did not offer her anything and it had been bothering me for years.

During college, my housemates asked me to apply for food stamps. I had used only a few stamps then as I did not cook. I feel ashamed as this is my only time to collect social welfare. We have regrets in life and we can only bring them to our graves.

The oil prices for the last 10 years from Nasdaq.com:

Home > Markets > Commodities > Crude Oil Brent

Crude Oil Brent

Latest Price & Chart for Crude Oil Brent

End of day Commodity Futures Price Quotes for Crude Oil Brent

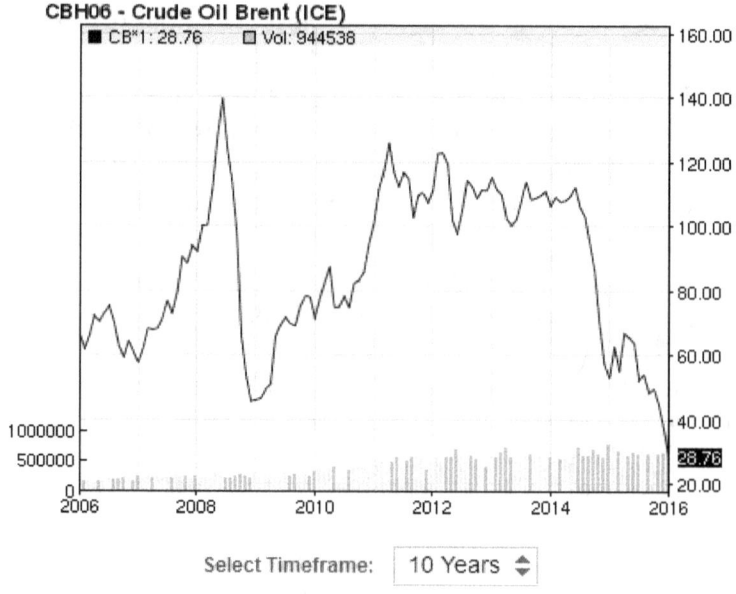

Select Timeframe: 10 Years

Crude Oil Brent Related ETFs: BNO

My predictions

Prediction #1. For the year, it will be in $25 to $40 per barrel. Personally I will not wait for a $25 rate as it may never materialize.

Reasons:

- Global economies have not recovered yet.

- Iran's oil will add more supply.
- OPEC and Russia cannot trim supply as their economies depend on oil export.

Prediction #2. For years later, it will return to $50 per barrel and be on its way to $100.

Reasons:

- Global economies will recover (they always do). But I do not know when that will happen.
- OPEC will trim their supply.
- Supply will be reduced due to the current cut back on drilling and exploration.
- Global population growth.
- Inflation (about 3% per year).
- Historical prices. Recently we had oil prices below $30 and then it went up to $140. Adjusted for inflation, the current price is even far less than $30.
- As a rough estimate (depending on individual oil fields), it takes about $50 to extract, market and explore one barrel of oil (i.e. the cost of goods).

  It is better to shut down many of the oil fields such as ocean fields and oil sands at today's $30 range. OPEC cannot cut due to the payments on the loans of many on-going ventures but they should in the future.

  To supply the oil with the depressed prices would be the same as spending all the money without caring about retirement.

Summary

It is a supply and demand play. It could also be a case of commodity dumping and the U.S. may try to protect its own energy industry – you may have heard it here first.

The Losers: OPEC. They tried to cut the price to bankrupt the shale energy ventures. You do not want to shake a baby too hard or drop a big stone on your own toe. Many will lose their jobs in energy fields and the railroad industry due to shipping less coal.

The Winners: Investors who buy at low prices now and wait patiently for the long term. I hope we're in this role. As history has shown, the crisis most likely will be a profit potential.

Oil and the market

Today the consumers benefit from low gas prices. Airlines benefit too if they have not hedged on fuels or are not forced to buy at fixed prices from foreign countries. However, the stocks tank with the fall of the oil prices, so the savings in driving for most of us is not worth it.

Some still argue that oil prices will go to $10. If it does, I will keep on buying. As from today's $28 to $10, you lose about $18 or about 65%. However, it has the potential to go back to $120 and that would be more than 400% return from $28 and 1,200% return from $10. I'm buying OIL, an ETN (similar to ETF) that is supposed to float with oil price. UWTI (3X leverage) can triple your money in either direction. I do not recommend UWTI as in one day it could wipe out your entire investment. Ignore the weekly fluctuations due to speculation by traders and look for the long term.

Usually falling oil price would benefit the market in general. However, falling too much as of today is not good for the economy. Usually the market is opposite of the oil price. Today it is an exception due to the oil producing countries including the Saudis and Russia dumping foreign equities to meet their obligations. I predicted that when the oil price is at $85 per barrel, then there will be less dumping of foreign equities and the high oil will affect the market (or the market will be in the opposite direction from the oil price again). The world economies are interconnected today better than before. When the U.S. market suffers, most other global markets suffer too. In addition, when there are major withdrawals from the U.S. funds, the fund managers have to sell their foreign holdings.

China cannot build storage fast enough. They need the oil as they're blessed with polluting coal but not with oil (even oil does not generate a lot of electricity). I recommend that China buys the futures of n years at y price. This will resolve the current fluctuations and bring back the market which would not correlate with the oil price. Some argued that oil prices have reached its peak and its average price is $35 for the last 70 years. He did not consider inflation. It is a big deal for 70 years – I remember I paid $1 for a Big Mac dinner 35 years ago and today it is about $7. He also did not consider all the easy oil has left – the oil that can be extracted without much drilling. Today the production cost for off-shore drilling or from oil sand is more than $35 per barrel.

There are many articles on this topic on oil. Just google "Oil Price". Here is one: 1.

Update as of 5/2016: Barron's prediction is mostly wrong as oil has passed $45 per barrel. It is due to unexpected events such as the fire in Canada.

I bought OIL in Jan. 19, 2016 (one of my purchases in this period). I expected it to increase in price by 50% as the oil does, but it only increased 25%. What happened to half of my profit? Consider USO as an alternative to OIL.

Expecting the oil price to appreciate, it is better to bet on oil service companies instead of OIL. Here is an article on how to play the oil commodity and a site on energy ETFs. I have the annualized returns of energy ETFs and CVX from Jan. 19, 2016 to May, 12, 2016.

Symbol	Description	Ann. Return
OIL	Crude oil	33%
USO	US Oil Fund ETF	112%
OIH	Oil services	80%
XOP	SPDR Oil & Gas	138%
IYE	iShr DJ US Energy	75%
XLE	S&P Energy	76%
CVX	Chevron	81%
Average		85%
SPY		32%

Exploring uranium

China will have 25 or so nuclear generators on-line by 2020, 4 years away from this writing. I hope it would give this metal a boost. With Japan's problem, uranium demand was at its historical low after inflation adjustment. We need to account for the old (more than 30 years) nuclear generators that will be decommissioned. However, the net gain is still substantial.

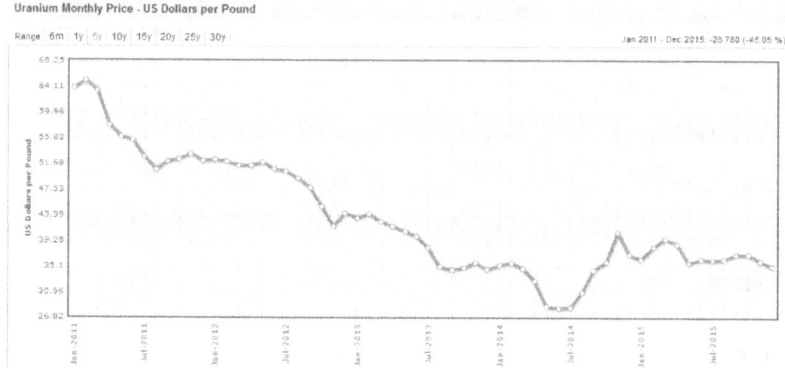

Source: Index Mundi

The price fell from 60 to 27 and rebounded to the current 35. The Monday quarterback would tell you to buy it at 27. Similar with oil, it is not unreasonable to double the price. The question is when. It could be 3 years or as high as 15 years.

Mining could be a different story as they need to survive from this depressed price. URA is the only ETF I can find with uranium and over 100 M. URA has many mining companies included. I will evaluate the companies in the future and at the current time frame, it is too risky for me.

An updated article on uranium.
https://seekingalpha.com/article/4252305-uranium-market-background-potential-investment-cameco

8   FAANG

To many, FAANG stocks define the market. To me, a conservative investor, it is not. For market-cap ETFs such as SPY, FAANG has more weight than other stocks. As a group, FAANG has been very profitable for the last year. To me they seem to be risky today. The following tables summarize them and I'll check them in a year and/or after September (usually the worst month) to confirm my findings. It is also a case of momentum vs. value.

All the info is available free on websites such as Finviz.com. All data is based on 8/5/2017. These are for info only and I'm not liable for any errors. Returns are annualized and dividends are not included.

Stocks	Current Price 8/5/17	From 8/5/16 to 8/7/17	From 8/7/17 to 8/7/18	From 8/7/18 to 10/7/18
FB	169.62	37%	7%	-84%
AMZN	173.85	29%	88%	2%
AAPL	156.39	48%	30%	48%
NFLX	180.27	48%	94%	-4%
GOOGL	945.79	17%	33%	-47%
Avg.[1]	247.41	44%	50%	-17%
Beat SPY by		214%[2]	233%	-440%
SPY		14%	15%	5%

[1] All averages in this article are estimates.
[2] Beat = (44% - 14%) /14=214%. Similar to other calculations for "Beat".

Fundamentals as of 8/5/2017

Stocks	P/E	P/E FWD	P/S	P/B	Debt/ Eq.	Sales Q/Q	EPS Q/Q	ROE
FB	37	26	15	7	0.00	45	69	23
AMZN	16	14	6	4	1.11	2	18	27
AAPL	18	15	4	6	0.73	5	10	35
NFLX	221	90	8	25	1.55	32	58	13
GOOGL	34	24	7	4	0.03	21	-28	14
Avg.	65	34	8	9	0.68	21	25	22
Beat SPY [1]	164%		277%	186%				
SPY[2]	25		2	3				

[1] Very rough estimates.
[2] Most fundamental metrics are from other source than Finviz.com, so there may be small discrepancy.

Technical as of 8/5/2017

Stocks	SMA50%	SMA200%	RSI(14)	52-week height	Short%	Insider Trans.
FB	8%	23%	67	-3%	1%	-86%
AMZN[1]	35%	8%	51	-6%	1%	0%
AAPL	5%	17%	63	-2%	1%	-31%
NFLX	10%	26%	59	-6%	6%	-69%
GOOGL[2]	-2%	8%	41	-6%	0%	0%
Avg.	11%	16%	56	-5%	2%	-37%
Beat SPY by [3]	1020%	173%	-9%			

[1] Recent double top. Bearish.
[2] Multiple top.
[3] Very rough estimates.
The two SMA (Simple Moving Averages) technical metrics are positive.

Summary

As a group, FAANG is fundamentally unsound but technically sound compared to SPY. I said the same on the market. As suggested, use trailing stops if you own any of these stocks. When they turn to be technically unsound, this is the time to exit. They could stay in the current valuations for a long time. However, when the institutional investors are dumping them, they will fall very fast and steep. SMA-20% would be a good indicator for an exit. NFLX is the most fundamentally unsound.

Update 8/7/2018. The rosy pictures of these stocks have been priced in. I recommend you sell the stocks with P/E over 35 unless you have a good reason not to. It is insurance to protect your profits. Even if they still rocket higher, you still will have a good sleep. When any bad news occurs, it would rocket back to earth. Newton's Law of Gravity?

9 Politics and investing

You may ask why politics is discussed in this investing book. Politics have been proven to affect the market. For example, the market had reacted to the different stages of Quantitative Easing whose dates had been preset. The following is a more recent example.

As of September, 2015, I predicted 2015 and 2019 would be profitable years even during the fierce correction in August. Why was I so sure? Very **seldom is the market down in a year before an election** including 2007. The last occurrence was 1939, the year when WW2 started. Investing is a multi-disciplined venture including statistics and politics. It may not always happen, but the probability is high for these years.

How to profit

2015 was a sideways market. The market reacted to good news and bad news. The strategy for a sideways market is: Buy at a temporary down and sell at a temporary peak. Define 'temporary' according to your risk tolerance.

For the 'temporary market down', personally I used 5% down from the last market peak. To me the 'temporary market peak' is 10% up from the last market down. The percentages can apply to the percentage changes in the stocks within your watch list. In other words, I buy the stock when the market is 5% down from the last peak and sell it when it gains 10%, or the market gains 10%. Be reminded that this strategy is opposite of market plunges, where you should exit the market totally - again depending on your risk tolerance.

The following are my purchases on 08/26/2015. I should have bought more stocks one day earlier if I were not blinded by fears (a human nature) during this correction. Below you will see my actual purchase orders. The four stocks were described as value stocks in an SA article and I did a simple evaluation. As of 12/31/2015, I sold all of the four stocks except Gilead Sciences. The annualized returns are more impressive such as GNW's 10% gain in one day.

Stocks	Buy Price	Buy Date	Return	Sold date
AAPL	107.20	08/26/15	12%	10/19/15
GILD	105.94	08/26/15	-4%	
GM	27.69	08/26/15	12%	09/17/15
GNW	4.54	08/26/15	10%	08/27/15

There were similar examples in 2013 and 2014.

2016: Politics and the market

No one including all the Federal Reserve chairmen / chairwomen and all the Nobel-Prize winners in economics can predict market plunges. One chairman predicted a smooth market and a few months later the housing market crashed! Many predicted correctly market crashes by pure luck. One even received a Nobel Prize and became famous. However, you would have been glad to ignore his later market predictions.

There are at least two best sellers asking us to exit the market in 2009. If you followed them, you would miss all the big gains from 2009 to 2014. They did have a point though. However, you cannot fight the Fed. The market had been saved by the excessive printing of money and hence created a non-correlation between the market and the economy. I bet these authors (famous economists and gurus) may have not made a buck in the stock market except selling their books or teaching where his students should request refunds. It is a classic case of the blind leading the blind, or diversion of theory and reality.

From their articles, they do not know the basic technical indicators. You only want react to the market when the market is plunging and not too early. That's why most fund managers cannot beat the market as most are not allowed to time the market. Buffett had mediocre returns in the last five years – I had warned my readers three years ago in my blogs/books. To me, the 'buy-and-hold' strategy has been dead since 2000. The average loss from the peak for the last two market plunges is about 45%. Most charts depend on falling prices, so you will not save 45% and a 25% loss is my objective.

Fundamentally speaking

The market in 2016 is risky due to the proposed interest rates hike (as of 4/15 the Fed indicated only .5% so it would not be a factor), our record-high margin, strong U.S. dollar (as of 4/15, it was weaker) and the high expenses of the wars. Each reason could be a good-size article. Personally I try to maintain 50% in cash and would flee the market if my technical indicator tells me so.

Politically (and statistically) speaking

The election year is the second best for the market, but it may not be this year. We **seldom** have three terms from the same political party. For that, I predict a win by the Republicans. Republicans are usually pro-business, but ironically the democratic presidency has a better track record for a better market performance.

The market has more than recovered since the day when Obama took office. The S&P 500 performance under Republicans vs. Democrats since 1926 to 2014 is approximately:

Annualized return under Democratic presidencies: 13%
Annualized return under Republican presidencies: 6%

The market is riskier based on the above statistics. In addition, there is a good chance that we will have either a non-politician president or a lady president for the first time (more materialized in 4/16). The market usually would not favor this kind of change. Statistics do not mean it will happen but history repeats itself more often than not in investing.

Critical political issue for 2016

On our way back at about 4 pm on a Saturday, the bus was full of Spanish-speaking workers. I bet most are illegal workers working in my suburb such as our malls, the hospital and many restaurants. Why illegals? I bet most legal folks would get welfare instead of working on that shift. If they work, the state would take away the freebies such as health care in many states. The illegals do not have this option. I do not think the politicians understand this. There is no need to build a border wall but rather punishing the employers who hire illegals. Before we do this, we need folks willing to take the jobs that are taken by the illegals today.

What will happen if the politicians allow all the illegals to be legal? There will be nobody doing these low-level jobs I predict. No one in his right mind wants these jobs when it is far easier to collect welfare. Why would politicians make this stupid decision? They want to buy Hispanic votes as evidenced in the last two elections.

In addition, most politicians side with the welfare recipients. Since 40% of the population does not pay Federal taxes, the politicians have to satisfy their needs in order to buy votes.

We should encourage folks to work. Representation without taxation is worse than taxation without representation.

Our high taxes, increasing minimum wage, regulations and strong US dollar dampen our competitive edge.

Some political decisions/regulations that affect the stocks

Beside the presidency and the interest rates hike(s), there are many political decisions and regulations that affect the stocks. Just to name a few here:

- The never-ending wars postpone our secular bull market beyond 2020.
- Solar City (SCTY) and this sector depend on government energy credit.
- My Chinese solar panel stock evaporated when the US banned them from importing them to the US.
- Any gun control measure will affect gun stocks (initially positive).
- When Hillary spoke against bio tech stocks or the coal mines, that sector sank.
- Restrictions on cigarettes if China and Russia follow our bans.

- Our immigration policy and great colleges attract the best from all over the world to come to the U.S. At the same time, we need to limit economical refugees from burdening our entitlement systems.
- France imposes extra taxes on foreign investors.
- Government bailouts on 'too big to fall' companies.
- High corporate taxes boost the exodus of corporate headquarters to tax havens outside the US.
- Infrastructure projects.
- Taking out the ban to export oil would increase the profits for oil companies.
- After the annexation of Crimea, the Congress restricted using Russia's rocket engines and gave some new opportunity to the US companies in this area. Besides political consideration, Chinese rockets are the most cost effective and more reliable.
- China's suppressing corruption affected Macau's casinos. Actually every major change in Chinese policy affects the world and global investors.
- Currently the policy of forcing Chinese banks to take stocks in failing companies makes me stay away from investing in all Chinese banks.
- As of 7/2017, the market has gained a lot since Trump's election especially those sectors fulfilling his election promises. Freddie Mac and Fannie Mac tripled after the election.

Summary

Politics affects the market. I predict a risky market in 2016.

Economy and religion also affect the market. Statistically speaking, the market is ahead of the economy by about 6 months. However, the current market is an exception due to the excessive money supply. The correlation will return to normal.

Religions in the Middle East have caused wars. These huge expenses are consumption, not investing. It will not be good for most sectors of the economy especially in the long run.

10   Winners / losers in a trade war with China

The following are based on my predictions on a full-fledged trade war with China. Buy the winners and short the losers. When the trade war is settled, reverse the directions. Losers are:

- American farmers and their suppliers such as fertilizers and farm equipment will be the chief losers. The government subsidies cannot last forever. Many have already lost their farms while their products have filled up storage spaces. Currently Brazil and Argentina are filling in the gaps to supply these products to China.

- Many chip suppliers to China will lose a lot of sales as China is the chief importer. It will take at least a year for countries to take up the slack. In 10 or so years, China will develop their own chip products. Hence, they will be back to normal in 2 years, and they will face China's competition in 10 or so years.

- Many U.S. companies are still profiting in China. These days are numbered.

- China in the future will reduce their number of buying new planes from Boeing and/or switch the orders to Airbus. Today China still needs a lot of new planes and hence the effect may not be immediate. China has the largest market for airplanes.

- Australia siding with the U.S. will be a serious loser. Australia supplies China with iron ores and agriculture products.

- Many Chinese companies especially Huawei will suffer a lot even with the help from the Chinese government. Huawei could lose their popular mobile phone sales outside China when Goggle stops suppling the apps to them.

- The markets in both the U.S. and China will fail. It could lead to a global recession.

- China would withdraw Treasury that could shake our reserve currency status of our USD.

- China would limit their export of rare earth elements to us.

Winners are:

- Vietnam is the obvious the largest beneficiary from this trade war. Many factories have moved from China to Vietnam. Many are owned by Chinese. China has helped Vietnam to improve their infrastructure. It has already gained about 8% of its GDP from the new business and is experiencing an influx of direct foreign investments.

- India could be a beneficiary too. They have a lot of problems to be fixed internally. They should copy the model of China by opening a special economic zone.

- Malaysia is a winner too. China will cut the rare earth elements to the U.S. Many countries including U.S. and Australia produce these elements but they do not refine them from the ores due to the damage to the environment. Most will be refined in Malaysia instead of in China.

- Countries may replace the U.S. as the chip and product suppliers to China. Taiwan and many EU countries are obvious beneficiaries. Many of them do not want to do business with China at the fear of being punished by the U.S.

- Russia will replace the U.S. as the supplier of energy such as LNG to China. They will have a closer tie than their history has shown.
- The South East Asia countries and some South American countries such as Brazil and Argentina will benefit and replace American agricultural products for China.
- Ericsson and Nokia will be the primary supplier of a 5G network to countries that ban Huawei's products. However, Ericsson's initial implementation is very poor compared to Huawei's.
- Many companies such as Samsung and Apple will capture Huawei's mobile phone market in Europe.
- More tourists and Chinese students will come to Europe particularly the EU countries.

Some of the symbols of the affected companies and country ETF are: VNM, INDA, EWT, ARGT, ERIC and NOK.

Book 2 (Bonus): Market Timing

There is no need to time the market from 1970 to 2000. From 2000 to 2014, the market crashed two times with an average loss of about 45%. Recently, the bull has been long (more than 10 years for the current one) while the bear has been less than 2 years. However, you may gain 10% or so a year in the bull market, while lose 40% or so in the bear market.

Using picking apples as an example, sometimes they may be sour but sometimes they may be tasty. The difference is picking them at the right time. It applies to market timing.

Market timing is about educated guesses. Hopefully we will have more rights than wrongs when we follow general guidelines. It would reduce risk and could benefit us financially in the long run. Recently we have had more false signals than the period between 2000 and 2010. However, it is better to follow a proven system. The harm could be minimal except for tax consequences as the system would tell you to return to the market briefly.

I divide the market timing in three categories by durations as follows. All time durations are estimates for discussion and all markets are different.

	Duration
Secular cycle	20 years (actually less)
Market Cycle	5 years (not the current one)
Correction: 10-20%	1 per year
5-10%	2 per year (count the above as 1)

Market plunges have losses between 30% and 55% usually. There is a gray area for the 20% to 30% losses, which does not happen often. When the market plunges, it plunges hard and fast. The techniques in this book tell you to exit the market and when to return to equities. The techniques are based on falling prices, so they will not indicate peaks and bottoms, but they will help you to reduce further losses.

Within the secular market, there are market cycles. There is a super cycle that I ignore as I find it not too useful Every market is different. Today we have excessive money printing that changes all the previous logic such as the average length of a market cycle. If the

USD is not the reserved currency, the market would fall. However, the correlation of the market and the economy will correlate again. We do not know when, but it will. Otherwise, we have to rewrite all the books on investing. For instant gratification, you can read Simplest Way to Time the Market and skip the rest of this lengthy section for now.

1   Market timing example

The market is making new highs as of this writing in early 2021. There are always two camps of market timers. One camp predicts a crash is coming while the other predicts it will continue making new highs. This article includes both arguments and suggests how and what actions you need to take to protect your investments. Be warned that all market is different and predictions are just pure predictions; the more educated the guesses, the more chance they will be materialized. In 2021, the market has been flooded with cash due to the excessive printing of money.

Management summary

The market is fundamentally unsound evidenced by fundamental metrics but technically sound evidenced by technical metrics that both will be described in this article. The data were obtained on 09/22/2018. This article shows you how to evaluate the market risk. As of 8/2021, the market has not changed a lot since 01/2020 with the following exceptions: 1.The excessive printing of money that is leading to inflation and 2. The pandemic is still not fully controlled.

Suggested actions
No one predicts the market correctly and consistently. Otherwise, there are no poor folks. Moving the risky investments such as most stocks to cash too early would miss the potential profits. Moving it too late would risk the loss of your stocks.

Your actions depend on your risk tolerance. If you are conservative such as a retiree, you may want to have a larger portion of your investments in lower risk such as CDs and bonds. You can take one of the following three actions or combine all of the three actions.

1. When the market turns to technically unsound, it is time to move your stocks to cash. The market timing indicators may give

false signals. In this case, the indicator would tell you to move back to stocks. Most likely you do not lose much except dealing with the consequences of taxes in non-retirement accounts.

2. Move a portion of your risky investments into cash, laddered CDs and/or short-term bonds. Again, the size of the portion depends on your risk tolerance.

3. Use stops. The sell orders would be changed to market orders when the stocks dip below prices specified by you. I prefer to use SPY or other ETF to determine the market direction. Some sectors and some stocks move faster than others. In one crash, my energy stocks were still profitable while the market was tanking. Eventually these energy stocks caught up and fell fast. Today's highly profitable stocks are FAANG stocks as a group.

I propose and prefer 'manual stop orders' to prevent market manipulation. However, usually large ETFs cannot be manipulated easily. Manipulators try to profit from your stop orders. Set a stop order price in your mind. When the stock falls to that specified price, sell it via a market order.

My friend confirmed my "manual stop order":

"High-frequency trading via Algo Trading Strategy can see exactly where pre-set trailing stops are and sweep across them (play them) like strings on a violin. Pre-set a trailing stop and it is bound to be triggered because Algo hunt them down. Then watch the market rip higher."

Analysis: Fundamentals and Technical

It consists of Fundamental Analysis and Technical Analysis. The former measures how expensive the current market is and the latter measures the trend of the market.

Many metrics were obtained from Finviz.com as of 9/22/2018 while others are obtained from other websites. With the exception of Fidelity.com, all websites described here are free and readily available. It also serves as a guide on how you can do your own market timing especially after a few months.

The following chart uses SPY to represent the market of the top 500 stocks. It is market cap weighted. It means the higher the market cap of the stock, the higher percent of the stock is represented in the index. It turns out most are riskier FAANG stocks. Enter Finviz.com in your browser and enter SPY. I am not responsible for any errors.

Indicator	Pass	Current Value	Indicating
• Technical			
Death Cross[1]		SMA-50 = 2.3% & SMA-200 = 6.3%	Pass
Technical Analysis: 350 SMA%[2]	>0	Price above the SMA-350.	Pass
RSI(14)	<70	61	Pass
Duration (yr.)	<5	10	Fail
		Overall	**Pass**
• Fundamental			
Valuation			
P/E[3]	<15.7	25.4	High by 62%. Fail.
Shiller P/E[3]	<16.6	33.5	High by 102%. Fail
P/B[3]	<2.78	3.52	High by 27%. Fail.
P/S[3]	<1.50	2.33	High by 55%. Fail.
Oil price	30-100	70.71	Pass
Interest rate[6] T-Bill 1 months[7]	<5	2.05	Pass
T-Bill 3 months[7]	Yield	2.18	
T-Bill 30 years[7]	Curve	3.20	Pass
Flow to Equity[4]		-3.371M	Fail
Flow to bond[4]		7.206M	
Corporate debt/GDP[8]	<40	45%	High by 13%. Fail.
USD[5]		Strong	Fail
Gold		High	Fail
Bubble		Several	Fail
Market experts		Fear long term	Neutral
Politics		Trump	Fail
Misc.		Trade war	Fail
		Overall	**Fail**

[1] This is the market timing technique without using a chart.

[2] I tried to use SMA-400% to reduce false signals without success.

[3] Get it from http://www.multpl.com/. Same as CAPE.

[4] Get it from https://www.ici.org/research/stats. It is based on 09-12-18. "Flow to Equity" is based on domestic ETF estimates. Treat it as two phases in moving to equity. First phase of moving excessively to equity indicates the market

is peaking. The second phase indicates the market is plunging when the flow of equity is excessively negative.

[5] Global corporations will suffer in profits converted back to USD and hard to sell to foreign countries.

[4] Get it from the above link.

[6] Rising interest is bad for corporations and high-ticket products, but good for lenders.

[7] Get it from https://www.treasury.gov/resource-center/data-chart-center/interest-rates/Pages/TextView.aspx?data=yield based on 09/21/18

[8] With the low interest rate, it may not be that critical. Corporations take advantage of the low interest rate.

Overall

Overall, technical is fine as the market is making new highs. Many aggressive investors exit the market on technical indicators only as the overvalued market could linger on for a long term such as from 2009 to 2017 so far.

Overall, fundamental is not sound. The increasing market price also is decreasing the fundamental metrics such as P/E, P/B and P/S. It is bad unless there is reason to support such as the fast earnings growth in 2009.

Many metrics are deteriorating

RSI(14) is getting closer to 65 (a passing grade specified by me).

Inverse yield curve (1.5 vs. 2.33) is about 61% apart from my interpretation and calculation. It is not a warning now but we should keep an eye on it. Most market crashes have occurred when it is 0% or negative. The theory is that in a normal case the short-term interest rates should be lower than the long-term interest rate.

Another source calculates it is 1.1% and that is very close to inversion since the last recession. From MarketWatch, the 30-year fixed interest rate is 4.66% and 1-year rate is 3.96% giving an inverse yield curve 18% apart, which is quite alarming.

Mathematically incorrect, today's full employment is at 4%. Most recessions are closely preceded by troughs in unemployment and the reverse for the economy to recover.

GDP growth has been predicted from 1.8% to 3%. The 3% is from the White House for their obvious purpose. I predict it will pop up due to meeting the tariff deadlines, tax cuts and spending increases. It will then be declining to 2%. A healthy US economy should maintain 3% without special factors such as excessive immigration.

We have record debts: investors' margin, corporate debt and Federal debt. These are bubbles going to burst. Federal debt / GDP is about 95% (https://fred.stlouisfed.org/series/gfdegdq188S) today. It does not predict the market performance as this ratio was 53% and 55% before the last two market crashes. It will affect the long-term performance of the economy when we have to service the huge national debt.

We do have 10 years of stock growth at the expense of a record Federal deficit. Thanks to President Obama from investors and no thanks from next generations who have to pay back our national debt. It is overdue for a correction. Hopefully it is not a crash which has an average loss of about 45%. We did have two recent corrections losing more than 10%: 2011-12 EU debt crisis and 2014-16 oil crash. The oil price has been rising from $30 per barrel to today's $70. It is still a long way from my warning of $120.

Potential triggers
Trade wars with China, Canada or the EU will be the strongest trigger. Our most profitable companies are virtually all international companies. They need fair trade to prosper.

The other trigger is the possible impeachment of President Trump.

Check the validity of our charts
It seems some metrics vary. It could be used after hour trading. It could be the "Days" may be "Sessions" – calendar day is different from trading sessions. I selected 10 years for most of the charts and StockCharts let me select only 5 years.

Here is a list of sites for charts.

https://www.stocktrader.com/2013/12/10/best-free-stock-chart-websites/
These are the three sites I use a lot: Fidelity (customers only), StockCharts and Finviz.com (missing some metrics).

As stated before, SPY may not be the best to represent the market. I prefer an ETF for 1,000 stocks and weigh the stocks evenly (i.e., not according to the market cap). Google "market timing 2020 (or current year)" for more expert info. Here is one.

Mid-year update

Basically, nothing significant has changed recently: The market is fundamentally unsound and technically sound after the recent rally. The only update is our national debt is skyrocketing. Today's "Debt/GDP" is similar to the market height in 2000 and we know what happened afterwards. That's why Buffett has accumulated a lot of cash now.

Even with the unlimited QE (i.e., printing money excessively), the high inflation and market crash predicted by many experts have not been materialized so far. This is my third prediction in "Disaster of 2020". The status of USD as a reserve currency will be shaken; I do not know when, as I do not have a time machine.

Why does the market keep going up while the economy is going down? The Fed has provided a lot of cash and the cash is chasing a fixed number of assets such as gold and stocks. It is the simple, proven theory of demand and supply. It will continue for a while as long as there is an unlimited supply of money. At some point, it will pop. At that time, it could lead to a long recession, unless the economy improves as it did in 2009. The smart Fed chairman knows how it will harm the country by excessively printing money. However, he has to obey his boss who is seeking reelection.

I expect we are in a prolonged period of low interest rates and even negative interest rates. When the rates are negative, our Treasury bonds are no longer marketable. The foreign central banks including China would dump our national debts if it has not already started. The economy is dressed up nicely in an election year. Giving us free money is the easy way to buy votes, but the long-term effects are very harmful.

Using cheap money to buy back the company's stock would boost the stock price and hence make the management wealthier. It is a false sense of the stock value. When the company cannot pay back the debt obligations, the company would go bankrupt. If the U.S. were a company, she would have gone bankrupt already.

As of 6/15/2020, QQQ (representing NASDAQ stocks) has been up 11% YTD and it is far better than DIA (representing DOW stocks) and SPY (representing the 500 large stocks in the S&P Index and losing about 5% YTD). QQQ has a lot of tech stocks while DIA has a lot of losers including Boeing. Most FAANG stocks are making record highs and QQQ is market cap weighted.

Most of the ETFs on chips have been up more than 40% in a year. I bought Amazon and two chip ETFs. I use trailing stops to protect my portfolio. Huawei is buying a lot of U.S. chips in the 120-day relaxed period. In September this year and if there is no extension, I would sell these chip ETFs fast.

I have used the strategy described in my book "Profit from the recovery of the pandemic" to take advantage of this volatile market. I used 5% as the threshold and I had too few trades; now I changed to 3%. Expecting a market crash, I weigh more on contra ETFs. As described in the same book, I bought a lot of contra ETFs, GLD and the stock of a gold miner. It is for insurance. Oil ETFs are my big mistake.

If the U.S.D. loses the status of reserve currency (not likely soon), it would bring prolonged depression and high inflation in the U.S. In this case, it is safer to invest in real estate, precious metals and profitable companies than in CDs and bonds that would lose value due to inflation.

Check out many articles on the status of the current market. Many have opposing views, so you have to make your own decision. In any case, play it safe with stops. Here is one article from MarketWatch.com.

Update 8/2021
Nothing has changed. The market is not sound fundamentally but fine technically. When the technical indicators tell us to exit, most

likely it is right. However, the market is volatile, and hence return to the market if the indicators tell us so. Here is an argument from opposite camps.
https://www.youtube.com/watch?v=I9P9IuwuTVE

Canary warning?
When I was working on my new book "Best stocks to buy for 2021" on Dec. 10, 2020, I found something really strange. I have never rejected so many stocks that have Fidelity's Equity Summary Score higher than 9. I rejected them as there was a lot of dumping from the insiders. Insiders know their companies better than most of us. Is it the canary telling us the market is overvalued?

Initially the following stocks have been screened by my value screens. Buy any one of the following stocks, **only** if you have good reason(s).

How can HEAR score a perfect 10 while the Insiders' Transaction is -75% (to me -2% is normal). The analysts must be wrong this time, or they believe the market will continuously make new heights.

Symbol	Fidelity Score	Insider Purchase	Return[1]	Annualized
BCC	9.9	-24%	46%	126%
GPI	10.0	-17%	35%	95%
HEAR	10.0	-75%	43%	118%
HVT	9.5	-37%	53%	144%
HZO	9.5	-27%	75%	204%
Average				84%
SPY				30%
Beat SPY[2]				177%

[1] From Dec. 20, 2020 to July 1, 2021. Fees, commissions and dividends are not included.

[2] = (Average – SPY) /SPY. SPY represents the market to many of us. This concludes the Insiders are wrong in this case.

A correction or a crash?
In Dec., 2018, the S&P 500 is about 15% down and a crash is about 45% down.

If a crash is coming, there should be an additional 30% down. If it is a correction (15% average), then we have it already. Should we pick up bargains now? Or, are they bargains? It is a trillion-dollar question.

We need a trigger for a market crash like the financial crisis in 2008 and the internet bubble in 2000. Besides the record-high margin debt, the possibility of Trump's impeachment and a trade war, I do not see any.

Links
Search articles from Google and YouTube on today's market conditions.
YouTube: 1
https://www.youtube.com/watch?v=czHUI0syjKo&t=300s

Filler: CIA mistook it as a missile silo in China.

Section I: Spotting big market plunges

1 *Spotting big market plunges*

This chapter is lengthy and complicated in some concepts; it also requires you to try it yourself. However, the result is far better. Make your market decision by combining all the hints described in this article. The first hint is the most important.

No one can consistently predict the correct stages of the market cycle. This chapter is intended for educational purposes only. However, if we have more rights than wrongs with our calculated and educated guesses, we should do well. As in everything in life, there is no guarantee.

These are my 11 hints to identify a market plunge. The average loss of market plunges from top to bottom for the last two crashes is about 45%. It could wipe out most gains for the entire market cycle. We target to avoid half of the loss.

Do not buy stocks during market plunge that could last for more than a year, which is defined by me from the market peak to the market bottom. It is a million-dollar decision for many including myself. This low-cost book serves as a reference and past performances do not guarantee future performances.

From 2000 to 2008, we only had one false signal for our SMA-350 out of 3 signals. Since then, we have had more false signals. To adjust to this volatility, do not move everything to cash on an exit signal. Adjust the amount of cash according to your own risk tolerance. Usually we do not lose much (sometimes we gain some) as another signal tells us to return to the market shortly. They only have tax consequences in taxable accounts.

Eleven hints of a market plunge

1. Technical analysis (TA).

The following chart is created by Yahoo!Finance. If it does not display well on a small screen, copy the following link to your browser to display it on your PC.
http://ebmyth.blogspot.com/2013/05/ta-graph-for-spotting-plunges-chapter.html

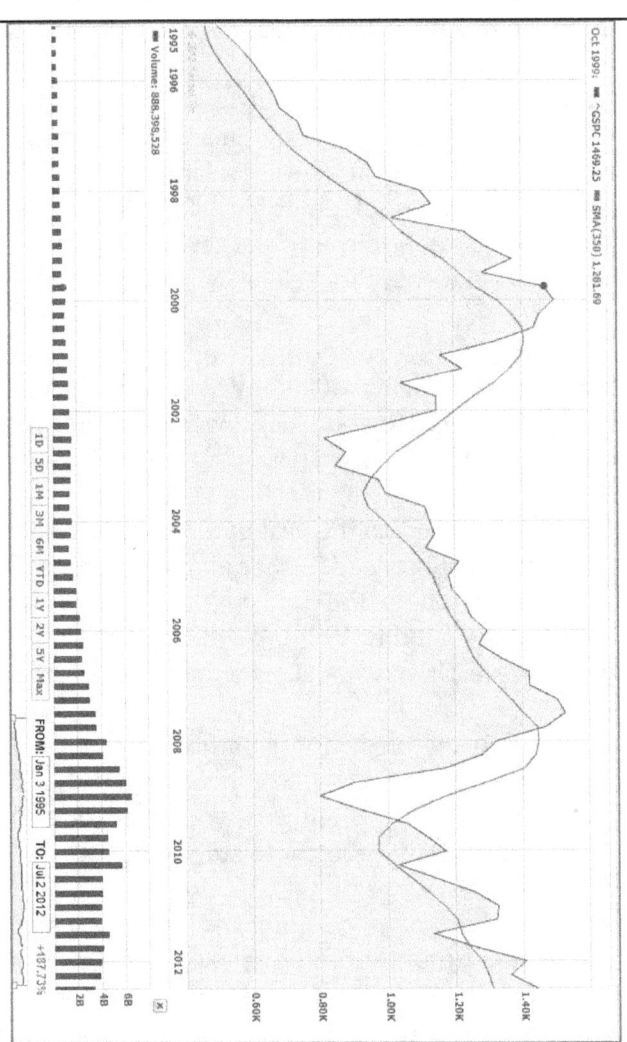

350 days simple moving average (SMA). Yahoo!Finance

The red line is the 350-day SMA, Simple Moving Average. If the stock price is below the moving average, it has detected a market plunge by this chart. Return to the market when the price is above the moving average line described as Early Recovery later. "350 days" are trading sessions. I have tried different "days" and 350 is the best fit for the last two market plunges, but it does not mean it would be the best fit for the next market plunge.

We have two cycles described in the chart. From the above, we should leave the market in the first quarter of 2000 and return to the market in the first quarter of 2003.

On the second cycle, the chart tells us to get out in Dec. 2008 and come back in July 2009 approximately. Enlarge the chart by selecting 5 years instead of the maximum or use a larger monitor for a more detailed chart. The chart sometimes gives false signals to tell us to exit but tell us to reenter briefly. In most cases, we do not lose much except the tax consequences for selling. No technical indicators are perfect.

I started to come back in Feb. 2009. It was perfect timing but most likely or partly it was due to good luck. I was partially influenced by several articles I read.

Technical Analysis is based on the past data, so you cannot avoid the initial losses but it could reduce further and larger losses. From the above, the chart detected the two big plunges nicely allowing enough time to take actions. Will the next plunge be detected? I guess it will. However, it may not allow enough time as the last two.

Sometimes, we time it wrongly or prematurely and miss some gains by leaving the market too early. We need to treat it as buying insurance; it only pays big when the worst happens. When the "reward / risk" is too low, it is better to stay in cash. One's opinion.

Return to equity when the price is above the moving average (the red line). You should profit more by following the chart than 'Buy and Hold' or keeping your money under the pillow. For the last two market cycles, I returned to equities in Early Recovery (a stage of the market cycle defined by me) and profited. Can I be 100% sure for the next market plunge and come back in a timely order? Certainly not.

If most of your stocks are in tech, use QQQ instead of SPY In addition, QQQ is more volatile than SPY and the tech sector usually leads the market.

It can be created by following the steps; you need to create one yourself to detect the next plunge with current data.

- From Yahoo!Finance or any chart systems, enter SPY (or the S&P 500 index) or an ETF that represents the total market.
- Select Interactive Chart.
- Click Technical Indicators.
- Select SMA (simple moving average).
- Enter 350 days (actually it is trade sessions). Many chart systems use 'month' as a unit, enter 12 or 11.67 if decimals is allowed (=350/12) instead of 350.
- Enter 1-3-2000 on "FROM:" or any "from date" that fits your screen.
- Select Draw.

Note. I switch to Fidelity for charting now as I cannot produce the same info from Yahoo!Finance. It could be my fault or a bug that should be fixed. If you cannot use Fidelity, try StockCharts.com.

---

2. Do the opposite of the flow of the dumb money.

When everyone is buying recklessly, making money and proclaiming that they are geniuses, sell. In 1999, my friend told me that he should quit his job and concentrate on investing as he was making many times in the stock market over his regular salary by spending half an hour a day. I would call myself a genius by making $1,000 an hour. When AAII's bullish sentiment (a contrary indicator to me) is over 70%, watch out.

In the same year, there were so many successful IPOs with '.com' names and these companies did not know how to make profits but blindly captured their market shares at all expenses.

They gave me $20 for just registering on their site. The poor quality of their ads showing their products during the Super Bowl reflected the quality of their management. The so-called 'MBA's business model' of capturing a potential market of one million potential sales by spending five million is not Business 101 but Fool 101.

The inverse flow of money market funds is a good indicator too. The more money flowing into the equity funds by retail investors, the riskier is the market. Greed is a human nature. It is hard to resist buying stocks when your friends are all making good money in the market and you feel you do not want to miss the boat. I tried unsuccessfully to convince lottery winners not to buy lottery tickets and they showed me they had made another thousand yesterday.

3. Duration.

Cycles usually occur every four or five years. This is a very rough estimate as cycles often vary from 1 to 8 or even more years. After the market plunge in 2007-2008, we are having (as of 12/2018) one of the longest bull markets. The longer it stays at the peak, the higher the chance the market will plunge and the further it will sink. I call it Newton's Law of Gravity or 'What goes up must come down'. When we follow the charts (technical indicators), we still stay in the market most of the time.

4. Valuation.

The average historical P/E of the S&P 500 is about 15 (or 16.5 depending on when you start the data). When it is over the average, be careful. Obtain the P/E of SPY (an ETF for the S&P 500) from Yahoo!Finance and confirm it in many other sources. When the average P/E of a sector is over 35, most likely there will be a fierce correction for that sector. When it is over 40, the market most likely has peaked. When you find fewer value stocks than before, it means the market is riskier now.

The P/E of the S&P 500 index was 28 in 2000. It was 18 in 2007 and 16 in 2015. Both are over 15, the average value for the last five years.

The value of the average P/E has to be adjusted as the market conditions are not the same 10 or so years ago. Today (2016) part of the earning (the E in P/E) is due to the low cost in borrowing and less wage cost due to hiring overseas. Most global corporations can offshore jobs to reduce expenses. The global economies are interconnected far better than before. When the global economies fall, we will fall too.

5. Triggers to burst a bubble.

In 2000, the trigger was the tech bubble. In 2007 it was the housing (or financing) bubble. It was easy to spot a massive tech bubble in 2000. I moved most of my tech sector funds to traditional sectors (cash for 20-20 hindsight) in the beginning of April, 2000, which was too close for comfort to this market plunge.

Most investors including myself did not understand the workings of the derivatives of the mortgage loans and could not recognize the bubble. I made good money in the oil sector in 2007. However, in 2008 most of my investments were losers including the investment in the oil sector. If I followed the hints described in this chapter, I would have avoided heavy losses.

6.   Rising interest rates.

It is more expensive for investors using margin to buy stocks, for companies to borrow money and for consumers to buy high ticket items and houses.

A related hint is rising margin debt (the debt used to buy stocks backed up by the current stock holdings). When we have a record of margin debt as in 2016, the chance of a market plunge is high when the Fed hikes the interest rates.

When the Fed discount rate is 5% or above, be careful. This is also the time to buy long-term bonds. When it is 1% or less, most likely the market starts to recover. This is also the time NOT to buy long-term bonds. This strategy was proven in market cycles in 2000 and 2008.

7.   Yield Curve.

When the short-term (say 3 month) interest rates are higher than the long term (say 30 years), it is abnormal and a bearish signal. Click here to check the yield curve.

Many use two-year Treasury and ten-year Treasury. As of Oct. 15, 2018, they were 2.82% and 3.09% and it was very close to being equal and gave us some warning of a potential recession. You may want to move some of your risky investments such as stocks to safer investments such as CDs and short-term bonds. As of 2018, only two false warnings from the last seven recessions when an inverted yield occurred. Again, your action depends on your risk tolerance.

http://www.treasury.gov/resource-center/data-chart-center/interest-rates/Pages/TextView.aspx?data=yield
http://blogs.marketwatch.com/thetell/2014/05/13/bear-market-wont-come-until-the-yield-curve-says-so-kleintop/

8.   Rising oil price.

It is the same as the above as rising oil prices will make everything more expensive. However, today (2015-2016) is an exception. The falling oil price correlates with the market. It is due to falling too much and the oil-producing countries have to dump the stocks to rescue their economies. If I have to put a number, I would say the market is risky when the oil price is below $30 or above $120.

9.   Market experts.

There are always two camps predicting the market trend. Check out those that make sense and ignore those who try to sell you books or their services. The media try to scare you to improve the circulation. The reason I exited the market in April, 2000 is the result of reading an article that said the entire company of an internet company could fit into a conference room of a company with the same market cap. Good seeds that fall on fertile soil will prosper. The opposite is true when bad seeds fall on poor soil.

10. Politics.

The long market rise from 2009 to 2016 is due to the low interest rates even though the economy is not doing well. The interest rate is controlled by the Federal Reserve Bank, which is an agent of the government. After WW2, the market has never been down in a year right before election. As of 2016, the low interest rate saved the market at the expense of our national debt which was at the recent peak. Trump's proposed 45% tariff could bring global recession starting in the US and China.

11. Miscellaneous.

In 2000, I exited the market after reading an article describing how the entire corporation could fit into a big conference of a large corporation. In 2008, we had a "<u>Double Top</u>" technical indicator that correctly told us of a market plunge.

Be conservative

As in any new strategy, test it out and try it out gradually with real money. Most of you paid less than $25 for this book and most likely you do not want to risk all your money based on a $25 advice, so consult your financial advisors. You should not lose money by exiting the market too early, but miss the opportunity to make more money. If the market does not crash, treat it as insurance. No one can predict market directions consistently and correctly. This article gives you better hints to time the market and all markets are different.

The chart worked fine for the last two crashes, but as in life there is no guarantee to detect the next market crash for the following reasons:

- It may not give us ample time to react as the last two. The current market is high and is caused by excessive money supply. When the money supply is reduced (or no more QEn), the market will react negatively.
- When too many folks buy my books and use the same chart, it will lose its effectiveness. It is most likely not, but there is always a chance.
- Past performances do not guarantee future performance.
- The market is not always rational.
- There are more noises (crossing the red line and backing again briefly) since 2011. The chart is not the only indicator I follow. Adjust it according to your risk tolerance.

Since 2011, there have been several exits/entries as the market is not rational. However, if you follow it, you're still faring well as they tell you reentry very quickly. You do not lose or gain a lot by doing so. Even if you lose a little, it could be the best insurance you bought.

The noises would be increased if we use 200 days in SMA in the chart instead of 350. For the same reason, they will be decreased if I use 400 days but the signal will be later delayed.

As in life, there is nothing guaranteed, the chart is far better than market timing without charts and/or no market timing at all since 2000. Start looking at the charts more frequently when you feel the market is risky.

Conclusion

This article provides my basic tools and my views on market timing. Market is not always rational otherwise there are no poor folks as stated before. When the market is about to plunge, run the chart more frequently and read more articles written by market experts.

Market timing is not an exact science but it is based on educated guesses. The better guesses should have more rights than wrongs in the long term. Your actions depend on your risk tolerance. Initially you should be careful on using any strategy that you do not have full understanding and enough proven record.

Technical analysis (SMA-350) is more important than fundamentals as an overvalued market could linger for years as in 2009 to 2017. Also recommend to read articles on experts on the current market. There are always two camps.

2 More tools

Using VIX as a timing model

When I overlapped VIX and the S&P 500 index, I found a consistent pattern. However, it has not been conclusive to me. Try to enter VIX in any chart system such as Yahoo!Finance with the S&P 500 overlaid. In the summer of 2008, VIX jumped about 500% from about 15 to 89.

VIX
http://en.wikipedia.org/wiki/VIX
VIX from Yahoo!Finance.
http://finance.yahoo.com/echarts?s=^VIX+Interactive#
There are several articles on the topic.
http://seekingalpha.com/instablog/434935-south-gent/3373095-vix-asset-allocation-model.
Ted Talk: 1
http://www.ted.com/talks/didier_sornette_how_we_can_predict_the_next_financial_crisis

Other technical indicators

- Head and Shoulder would predict a market plunge as evidenced in 2007. The reverse pattern would predict a market surge as indicated in 2009.
- Double Top is a bearish signal and double bottom is a bullish signal.
- Death Cross is used to detect large plunges and it does not require charting via Finviz.com. Golden Cross detects when to return.
- MACD (Moving Average Convergence Divergence). When the indicator is below the zero line, it is bearish and vice versa. Use it as a secondary indicator to detect the market direction.
- When RSI (14) is over 65%, the market is most likely overbought (i.e., overvalued).
- Use the following SMA-20 as a secondary indicator as an alternative to the SMA-350. When the stock price is below SMA-20 (Single Moving Average for the last 20 sessions) for three consecutive days, it indicates a possible market plunge. In theory, the institutional investors dump the stock on the first day and then the retail investors follow on the second day. If it

continues on the third day, most likely it is not the trick of the institutional investors to take advantage of the retail investors.

Sound Advice Risk Indicator

We only invest in stocks or real estates in a crude sense. This indicator comparing the allocations between these two investments has been quite successful. When we invest too much in the stock market instead of real estate, we will expect a market crash. When this index hit 2 as in 1906, 1928, 1937 and 1965, we had market crashes at all these times. Today (12/2018), we have a similar warning. Use Google to search for articles mentioning this indicator. Here is one of many.

Buffett's Equity to GDP

It measures the value of the market. It has been quite successful. Google for the current value. Advisor Perspectives may have this value and many insights on the current market. It will not detect the peaks and bottoms as no one can consistently. About a third of the earnings of the S&P 500 companies come from abroad. Hence it boosts market cap but doesn't include those countries' GDP. This is a major fault.

https://www.youtube.com/watch?v=dexOhg3pYa0

3   Related topics

Other related hints on value

The oil and industrial commodities (copper, steel...) are within 20% of their record highs. From my memory, it is the first time that oil is in sync with the market due to the dumping of stocks by the oil-producing countries today.

The total market cap is higher than the GDP. As of Nov., 2013, "Market Cap / GDP" is about 110% (fair value at 85%) and hence it is overvalued. Daily ratios can be obtained from GuruFocus.com, a paid subscription service. It does not work in the current cycle from 2008. It may be today because most large companies are multinational. However, today most large companies are global companies, so it loses some luster in using this ratio.

Dow Theory and many similar market timing strategies may become less effective as every market is different. Many ignore the service industries such as selling music and games via downloading.

From my observation, the higher the interest rates are, the higher the chance that a market plunge will be. The companies will have less earnings due to the higher borrowing costs especially in businesses that require a lot of borrowing and/or most of their customers' purchases are via financing. The stocks are more expensive to buy using margin accounts. Hence, the market will not fare well when the Fed hikes the interest rate.

Q including intangible assets is with P/E in evaluating the value of the market. It is harder to calculate.

Shiller P/E (same as CAPE or PE10)

It can be used to detect the valuation of the market. The P is the S&P 500 (or use SPY) and E is the average earnings of the last 10 years. It can also be used on sector ETFs and stocks. Use it as one of the hints. The major flaw is 10 years is too long of a time.

To simplify, most likely the market valuation is low (good to buy) when the P/E is below 15. The market valuation is high when it is above 20. As of 2014, it is far above 20 (17 in 2/2016). CAPE (cyclically adjusted price/earnings ratio) is available from the web by searching "CAPE P/E" to get the current reading.

Shiller's P/E   http://www.gurufocus.com/shiller-PE.php
From the above links, CAPE has been pretty decent. The reason why it does not work in 2014 is the excessive money printing that makes the market not act rationally. Treat it as a secondary yardstick at best. Here is a good article on P/E and PE10.
https://www.advisorperspectives.com/dshort/updates/2016/11/0
1/is-the-stock-market-cheap

He has been wrong since 2011 for calling recession every year. Here is his 2020 prediction. A best seller has been preaching similar ideas of bubbles since 2009.

Fear and Greed

This index from cnnFn.com is a similar contrary index. Leave the market when Greed is high and vice versa.

Many high-flying internet stocks lost more than 95% of their peak values. As in any bubble, the last ones to get into the bubble suffer most. The investors make out pretty nicely if they use the strategies below:

- Use a stop loss to protect your profits. Periodically adjust the order when the stock appreciates.
- Use SMA-20% (from Finviz.com). When the stock falls below the Simple Moving Average for the last 20 sessions, sell it. Use SMA-50 instead if you have a higher risk tolerance.

Lazy man's market timing
Sound Advice Risk Indicator, Equality to GDP, Inverted Interest Curve and Death Cross make up the lazy man's market timing. Google for the current values of the four. If you cannot get the last one, calculate it from Finviz.com.

Fidelity
From Fidelity.com, click on "News & Research" and then "Stock Market & Sector Performance" for Equity Market Commentary.
My experiences
I did not time the market seriously until 2008.
- 2000 Exit. I moved most of my sector funds (most in tech) to traditional sectors after reading articles on how overpriced the internet stocks were. It would be more profitable if I moved them to cash. They did not have contra ETFs then. I could not short stocks in my retirement accounts and I did not have experience in options.
- 2003 Return. I bet the market would return in two years. I bought many stocks which could survive in two years with the cash they had. I was lucky that the market returned in the same year. One stock was acquired by IBM with a huge gain.
- 2008 Exit. I did have the chart but I did not follow it. My big wins in energy stocks in 2007 gave me false security. When the market crashed, the energy stocks crashed too. I sold some stocks during the crash. I should have bought contra ETFs.
- 2009 Return. My chart told me to return in mid-March, 2009. I started buying in Feb., 2009. With the accumulated short-term capital losses, I traded stocks. I used my home equity loan that

has far lower interest rates than my margin account – not recommended. I used the margin account only to fill up the gaps between trades. Most of the time, the margin and the loan were zero. It could be my best year with making about 80% profit in my largest taxable account.

- Search the current YouTube video for "Market Sense" or search it within Fidelity.

False alarm

From 2000 to 2010, there is only one false alarm. From 2011 to 2016, there were more false alarms. We can change the parameter from SMA-350 to SMA-400 to reduce the number of false alarms at the expense of detecting the plunge a little late. The market before 2000 is quite different from the market today. Hence, I do not use the data before 2000.

4   Why the market fluctuates

The following chart uses SPY (simulating the market) with SMA-350 for the year of 2020 using Fidelity's charting function. It will be used to demonstrate how SMA-350 worked for 2020; the dates may be several days off. This article is written on 1/1/2021.

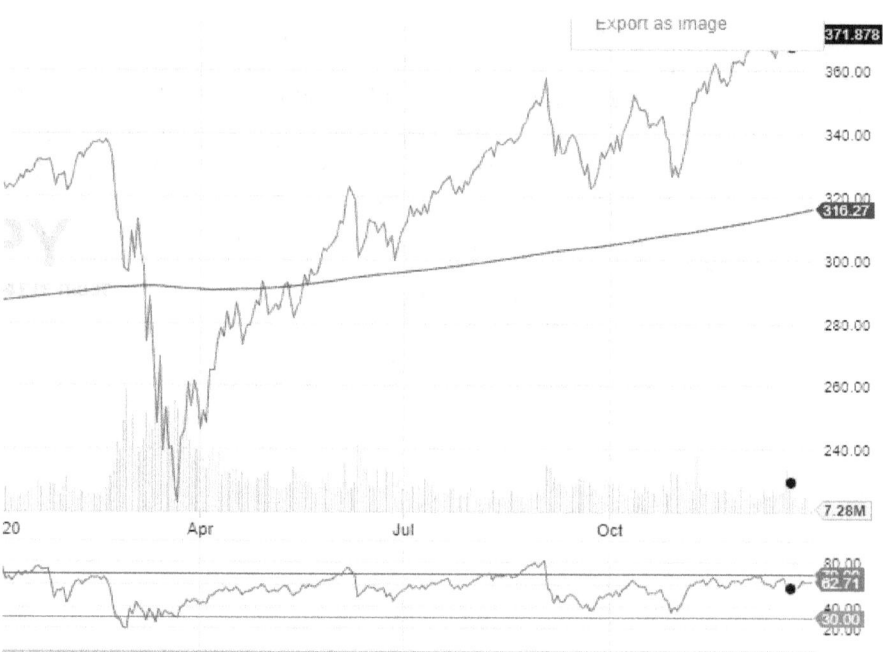

Market Timing

SMA-350 (Simple Moving Average for the last 350 sessions), described in this book, worked fine in 2020. It told us to exit the market on about 3/11/2020 and return on about the beginning of June. There were two false signals (on about 4/28 and 5/8) that told you to exit but return to the market shortly.

The other indicators are RSI(14) and P/E. Fidelity's chart uses 80 for overbought and 30 for under-bought for RSI(14). The market has been overpriced for a long while. In this case, technical analysis (SMA-350 I used in my example) works better than fundamental (P/E as one of the metrics); It has been sold for the entire 2020.

Why there is a big drop in late March and why it comes back

The trigger is the pandemic.

The market came back for many reasons:
- We understood the pandemic better.
- A lot of money on the sideline.
- The government supplies more money by printing it excessively.
- The government lowers the interest rate (almost to zero).

2021 prediction

It is quite hard to predict the market. Here are my thoughts. The market is not rational (fundamentally speaking).

For:
- The government keeps on excessively supplying money.
- With easy credit, the rising housing market leads to many profitable sectors such as furniture.
- Due to easy credit and recovery, many companies buy back their own stocks.
- Low margin interest rate usually boosts the stock market.
- If the vaccines can control this pandemic, many sectors will recover. As I demonstrated before, we have to wait one more year for some sectors such as airlines, restaurants and cruise lines.
- Trade war with China could be reduced under Biden.

Against:
- The pandemic has not been stopped.
- Unemployment is breaking the previous record.
- Small businesses continue to go bankrupt.
- Complete decoupling with China.
- The government tools do not work anymore such as lowering interest rate.
- Super inflation is due to ample supply of money chasing a fixed amount of assets (stocks for example). It would also shake the status of the USD as a reserve currency.

As in any market, there are two camps opposite to each other. Need to watch the market like a hawk and take actions accordingly (talk to your financial advisor first). I expect the plunge would cause the market to lose about 40% if it happens.

5   Double tops & a faster indicator

The following is the chart to use <u>double tops</u> to detect the last market peak in 2007.

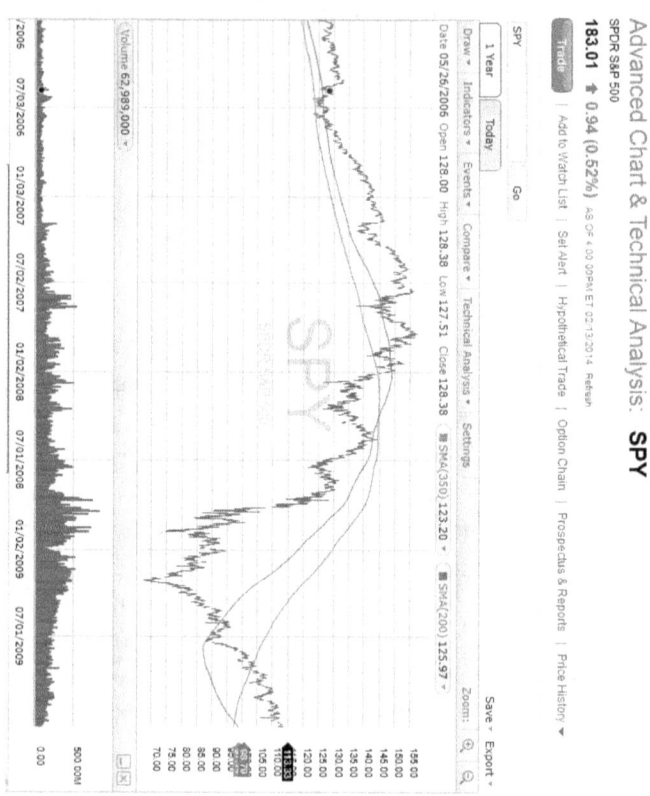

SPY: SMA.   Source: Fidelity

If you have a small screen on your e-reader, produce a similar graph using Yahoo!Finance. Enter SPY and select Technical Indicator. Select SMA and 350 days. Select the date from 1/3/2006 to 1/3/2010. Do another graph with SMA-200 as an overlay.

Critical dates

Table: Vital Dates

Market Plunge	Peak	Bottom	Indicator Exit	Indicator Reenter
2007	10/12/07	03/06/09	01/03/08	09/08/09

The following were obtained from my naked eyes to obtain the data from the graph. They are not accurate but are fine for discussion.

Top	Date	SPY
First	07/17/07	155
Second	10/11/07	157
Difference	86	1%
Selected	10/11/07	
Peak	10/12/07	

The SMA-350 indicator suggested us to exit the market on 01/03/08, about 83 days past the peak (10/12/07). Double Top is a better indicator here as it told us only one day before the peak. Will it happen again? Only time can tell.

Double Bottom

Again, the following is from my naked eyes to obtain the data from the graph.

Bottom	Date	SPY
First	03/17/08	127
Second	07/15/08	122
Difference	120	-4%
Selected	07/15/08	
Bottom	03/06/09	

Arbitrarily, I use the absolute difference of 5% or less to determine the double bottom condition (the absolute % of the second bottom to the first bottom).

The SMA-350 indicator suggests us to reenter the market on 09/08/09, about 186 days past the bottom (03/06/09). Double Bottom tells us to reenter the market about 234 days after the bottom. Hence, double bottom as defined here is not a good indicator.

It is interesting that the difference of days is 120. If we use 100 days as the threshold, then it is not qualified to be a double bottom.

We may want to use the earlier of either the chart or the double bottom to determine when to reenter the market.

Is SMA-350 better than SMA-200?

From the graph in this article, I conclude that SMA-200 has more noise that tells you to exit and reenter (or the other way) more often than SMA-350. It is logical as SMA-350 uses a longer duration (350 days vs. 200 days) for the moving average.

However, SMA-200 tells you to reenter the market earlier from the actual bottom in my limited tests. Hence, it is more profitable at least for the market plunge in 2007. For the next plunge, I would use SMA-350 to exit the market and SMA-200 to reenter the market. Is it just coincidental?

A faster, confirming indicator

In case you do not exit the market on the first sign, another faster technical indicator (SMA-50) would confirm the market plunge when it crosses over the SMA-350 downwards on Jan. 18, 2008 as an indicator in the following graph. The reentry using cross-over does not fare that well as expected.

In addition, high volume (compared to the average volume is a confirmation. To illustrate, if today's volume of SPY doubles its average daily volume, then it is a good confirmation.

Link
Double Tops:
http://www.investopedia.com/terms/d/doubletop.asp
Double Tops Video.
https://www.YouTube.com/watch?v=b-PaSDJiG2U

Illogical English

How can you "flying on a jet plane" (only Afghans can do so, which is a sad joke)? It should be "in". Did Peter, Paul and Mary screw it up?

6   Retail investors and market timing

The average retail investor has advantages over the fund managers. However, the average retail investor does worse than the market. They buy high and sell low - a kind of herd mentality.

In quarterly summaries, Fidelity demonstrated this more than one time. It shows that most retail investors moved their stocks to money market funds when the market was at temporary bottoms (or close to it), and moved them to equities when the market was at temporary peaks (or close to it).

It could be a good contradictory indicator if Fidelity or any fund company publishes this money market flow.

Morningstar has similar proof. From 2000 to 2010, equity funds earned an annualized return 1.6% while an average investor captured a .2% return due to moving in and out of the funds at the wrong time.

From my own observation, investors' sentiment works in the short term, but not in the long term.

It makes 'Buy and Hold' look great. The best strategy is 'Buy at the bottom and sell at the top'. It is easier to preach than practice. Can we overcome the human nature of 'Fear and Greed'?

The majority of retail investors do worse than the market and so are most fund managers. Logically, a group of investors must beat the market. They are the institutional investors besides the fund managers. We try to be as good as this group. It is achievable if you read the chapters on market timing, stock selection and strategies in this book. Most institutional investors do not time the market and we, the retail investors, have an advantage.

Do not act right away on the financial news you hear. A lot of the time, they're contradictive, sometimes manipulative and always too late to be useful. Reading WSJ or Baron's is more useful.

Cramer will tell you how the market is manipulated.
https://www.YouTube.com/watch?v=GOS8QgAQO-k

Afterthoughts

- Searcher said:
  Guess it is a given that I, as a proxy for the average investor, am very likely to buy high and sell low because I become giddy, or at least complacent, at higher highs and frozen with fear and indecisive at a declining market until the psychic pain forces capitulation. Should I have the good fortune to encounter this article and divest, I'm not sure that I'll have the same fortune to overcome my fear and general malaise in avoiding a bear 'fake out'. Thus, riding the market up looking for confirmation until, guess what? I'm buying at the top.

- Clay said:
  In my nearly 40 years in the investment mgt. arena, I find that a very small percent sell at the tops and buy at the bottoms and it is the same ones over and over. The long-term investor, from my experience, has been the clear winner in holding good stocks through thick and then. The trader may miss a bear market, but usually leaves very early, and comes back in very late. There's the formula for subpar performance.

- DanT, an x-stock analyst, said:
  The retail investor has every advantage over the institutional investor. You might not know just how right you are. Needless to say, it's also true that many retail investors (especially untutored ones) shoot themselves in the foot by reacting emotionally to market fluctuations. To augment what you said about Fidelity's research regarding money markets, did you know that under Peter Lynch, most of Fidelity Magellan's shareholders in fact lost money during Mr. Lynch's tenure? Guess how they lost it -- selling low and buying high.

  Very dubious am I, however that anyone can time the market, and the more confident one is in one's self-regarded timing "skills" or the level of technical research they engage in, the greater the danger there is. For the individual investor - any individual investor - it's the best answer to the vicissitudes of the market, in all applications.

The trick then, if you're still concerned with buying at too high a price, is to scale back during boom times and establish more conservative positions while throwing a little more money around after panics or flash crashes. The problem many people have, I've found, is that the money burns a hole in their pocket and they lack the discipline to maintain a cash reserve. A cash reserve isn't sexy, you can brag about the returns you get on your money market or savings acct..., but when you can scoop up a few thousand shares of XOM after the Dow falls a few hundred points, you feel better about it.

- With skills in market timing, one can beat the 'Buy and Hold' strategy. However, for the majority, 'Buy and Hold' is not a bad strategy.

- The retail investors moved billions to cash in 2009, the market bottom. Who are the lucky buyers? Institutional investors of course and hopefully my readers next time!

Links

Old links with the basic ideas never fade.
Advantages:
http://www.tonyp4idea.blogspot.com/2011/11/no-more-investing-hero.html
Herd mentality:
http://www.tonyp4idea.blogspot.com/2011/12/fool-of-all-fools.html
Psychology 101:
http://tonyp4idea.blogspot.com/2012/01/investing-psychology-101.html

Fillers

Cocktail parties in 1999
I had a hard time convincing my friends and coworkers in 2000. How can you tell the lottery winners not to buy lottery tickets? We do have many rocket stocks today. From my books, I recommend you use trailing stops.

Section II: Market cycle

1   Market cycle

"Bull markets are born on pessimism, grow on skepticism, mature on optimism, and die on euphoria" - Sir John Templeton

The stock market has cycles as our practical interpretation of the above. It is about five years apart, but it fluctuates widely. I divide it into four stages: Bottom, Early Recovery, Up and Peak.

My defined four stages of a market cycle

We need to apply the right investing strategies to each of the four stages of the cycle.

- **Bottom**

    I would not invest for at least the first six months (or even a year) after the big plunge starts, which could lose over 25% in a few months. The exceptions are investing in contra ETFs and selling short for aggressive investors.

    I estimate it will take a year from the start of the plunge to the bottom, so I will normally sell stocks early in the plunge and do not buy stocks that are in the sector (sometimes sectors) that cause the bubble for about two years after the plunge.

    At the bottom, the high-yield corporate bonds (i.e., junk bonds) would prosper when the interest rate is decreasing to stimulate the economy.

    From mid-2007 to mid-2008, bonds suffered as the investors thought the sky was falling down - it was to those who lost their jobs and/or their houses. After that, some bonds, especially the long-term bonds, could appreciate about 50% in the following year.

    The government lowered the interest rates and these bond prices with high interest rates surged. Correct timing in buying bonds could be very profitable.

Long-term bonds have more impact by the interest rate: The lower the interest rate, the higher the bond prices of higher-yield bonds. The older bonds with higher interest rates are more valuable to the newer bonds with lower interest rates.

I define this period of the bottom from the start of the plunge to the start of Early Recovery.

- **Early Recovery**
It usually starts after one year from the plunge; no one can pinpoint the exact time consistently. By this time preferably earlier, we should have closed out all positions in contra ETFs and shorts.

Roughly speaking, October, 2007 (some use 2008) is the start of the market plunge. March, 2009 is the end of the bottom stage and the start of the early recovery stage of the 2007 cycle. However, every market cycle is different in where it starts and ends.

The one-year gain from the bottom is most profitable. It usually gains over 25% in a year from the market bottom. I, a conservative investor, had huge gains using some leverage in my largest taxable account in 2009. From my memory, I had a similar return in 2003 but I had not saved the statement as in 2009.

In this phase, value is a better parameter than growth in searching for stocks. If your investment subscription provides a composite value score and a composite timing score, the sort parameter of your screened stocks could be "Composite Value / Composite Timing" in descending order. Select the top stocks in this order. You still have to analyze the top-screened stocks.

Forward (same as Expected) P/E is a good metric. However, most companies may be losing money at this stage. Those companies that can last for more than one year with its cash reserve are potential good buys. The best appreciated stocks are beaten companies that have precious technologies and good customer bases. They could be candidates to be acquired if they are small enough.

- **Up**

  Usually, the growth metrics such as PEG could be better than the value metrics such as expected P/E during this phase. Most stocks are winners except contra ETFs and shorting stocks. When the growth stocks are making headlines and the defensive stocks are being dumped, this is the hint that we're well into the Up phase of the market cycle.

  Locate stocks with growth metrics such as favorable PEG and high SMA-200% (from Finviz.com). Do not be scared of how much they have already appreciated. The strategy "Buy High and Sell Higher" works in this phase. Protect your profits with stops.

  Ensure that they have value too. Skip the stocks with expected P/Es higher than 35 unless there are good reasons. Most stocks will gain due to the tide of the market. However, when they're overbought (RSI(14) over 65), be careful. When institutional investors sell these stocks, they will crash.

- **Peak**

  When everyone makes easy money and the interest rates are high, watch out. Stop loss and/or stop limit should be used to protect your investment. Check out whether there is any bubble that would burst like the internet in 2000 and finance (and housing) in 2007.

  The internet crisis is easy to spot, but not the financial crisis. In 2007 we had a cycle longer than the average which is about 5 years. The plunge is very fast and very steep – thanks to the institutional investors who drive the market down.

  Run the technical analysis chart described in the Chapter on Spotting Big Market Plunges at least monthly (weekly if you have time). Protect your investment. Do not fall in love with any stock (you can buy it back later at a deep discount). Making the last buck is a fool's game.

Accumulate cash according to your risk tolerance. A retiree or a conservative investor would accumulate from 25% to 50% and should be ready to move to all cash when the plunge starts.

We can lower the cash percent if we use enough stop loss protection. Be psychologically prepared because the stock market may still rise for a while. There is no perfect market timing.

The 2007 Cycle

The market plunged starting in 10-2007 and ending in 3-2009 (bottom), started to recover in 3-2009 (early recovery), and trended up from 2010 to 1-2013 (the up phase of the market cycle). As of 3/2016, it is the peak phase defined by me.

As of 1/2013, we have recovered all the market losses since 2007. However, as of 7/2014, the economy has not fully recovered compared to the economy before the plunge. The employment judging by the medium salary has not fully recovered and the economy is not expanding. It is uncommon that the economy does not follow the market. It is due to the excessive supply of money by the government and partly due to globalization to allow companies to hire overseas.

Although a W-shaped recession seldom happens, we have a chance today. We hope we do not have a depression and/or the similar lost decades that Japan has been experiencing. Some may conclude we are close to completing a market cycle from 2007 to 2016. As of 2016, the economy is recovering slowly and we're better than most other global economies.

Again, market timing is not an exact science as it involves irrational human beings and government interventions. The timing using the market cycle described here is a guideline as it is hard to time it exactly.

The average market cycle is about 5 years, but they fluctuate. If we consider 2007 as the plunge, we have about 8 years of this cycle as of 2015.

In a typical cycle (few are typical), we have about one year in each of the 4 phases I defined (plunge, early recovery, up and peak).

Events/Triggers

There are financial events and triggers that cause the transition of one phase of the market cycle to another. They usually do not change the sequence of the phases (say not from Peak to Early Recovery), but they may change the duration of the phase. Examples are:

- The government announcing change of the interest rate,
- Change of employment, and
- Change of GNP.

Sectors in a market cycle (my suggestion)

Market Phase	Favorable		Unfavorable
Early Recovery	Financial, Technology, Industrial		Energy, Telecom, Utilities
Up	Technology, Industrial, Housing		
Peak	Mineral, Health Care, Energy, Long-Term Bond, Consumer Discretionary		
Bottom	Consumer Staples, Utilities		Consumer Discretionary, Technology, Industrial, Long-Term & high-yield Bond

The sectors that cause the recession usually take a longer time to recover. In 2000, the technology sector was not favorable in the Early Recovery phase, contrary to the above table. In 2007, the financial sector was not favorable in the Early Recovery phase. These are the "offending" sectors that cause the plunges.

In a recession, we usually cannot cut down on consumer staples and utilities, but we can cut down on buying consumer gadgets. Companies usually postpone investing in equipment and systems during a recession and expand when the economy is humming. The government usually lowers the interest rates right after the plunge to stimulate the economy.

Conclusion

When the market is about to plunge or change from one stage to another, run the described chart more frequently and read more articles written by the experts.

Again, market timing is not an exact science but it is based on educated guesses. The better guesses should have more rights than wrongs in the long term. Our actions depend on our risk tolerance. Be careful of using any new strategy that has not been fully understood and proven. Since 2000, market timing is very important to your financial health with two market plunges with an average of about 45% loss.

Afterthoughts
- The Dow Theory has a lot of followers in detecting market directions. In a nutshell, the market heading upwards is confirmed by the Industrial Index and the Transportation Index (less important in today's market especially with internet sales such as songs and movies), and vice versa. As of 4/2014, the two indexes are not in uniform.
  http://finance.yahoo.com/blogs/talking-numbers/this-is-a-130-year-old-warning-sign-for-stocks-231901097.html

- The bear market has the following three phases.

1. The market is overvalued.
2. Corporations are not doing well with decreasing earnings and sales.
3. Investors are selling due to fears.

  It is the reverse for a bull market: 1.The market is under-valued. 2. The market increases due to increasing corporate profits/sales and 3. Investors are buying due to greed.
- Investopedia has several articles on this topic.
  http://www.investopedia.com/terms/b/businesscycle.asp

- The yield curve could predict the interest rates change and hence the economy. There are three main types of yield curve shapes: normal, flat and inverted.

  A normal yield curve is one in which longer maturity bonds have a higher yield. Similarly, the long-term CD should have a higher interest rate than the short-term CD.

  When the shorter-term yields are higher than the longer-term yields, it indicates an upcoming recession. A flat yield curve indicates the economy is transiting. Now, you've read the essence of a book on this topic costing about $50 to buy.

  However, especially today, it does not mean anything as the government supplies too much money to stimulate the economy unsuccessfully. My simple chart described using SMA-350 (Simple Moving Average for 350 trading sessions) which depends on the stock price works better. Click here for "The dynamic yield curve" (http://stockcharts.com/freecharts/yieldcurve.php).

  The interest rate plays a role too. The easy money encourages folks to borrow money to buy stocks and companies to acquire other companies.
- As of Feb., 2013, I believe we're in the Up stage of the market cycle. I checked the performances of my top screens from each stage (a.k.a. phase) of the market cycle for the last 60 days. The best performance as a group belongs to the screens for the Up stage. Controversial! Always use the screens (same as searches) that perform well recently.

  In addition, the market has recovered 120% of the loss of 2007-2008. Hence the duration for an average Up stage of the market is quite close.
- Total Market Cap / GNP ratio is hotly debated on the market value. Different from the traditional 100%, I would suggest that the boundary ratio should be 130%. If it is over 130%, the market is overvalued and vice versa.
  http://www.investopedia.com/terms/m/marketcapgdp.asp

Market cycle: https://www.youtube.com/watch?v=ebWL2TrIssA

2   Actions for different stages of a market cycle

There are different strategies for the different stages of the market cycle.

Strategies during market plunges

The market plunge is defined as the period between the market peak and the market bottom. It usually lasts for one year or two.

When you spot the potential plunge, consider the following actions. It depends on your risk tolerance and your investment style.

1. Contrary to popular belief, parking cash is a strategy too. Cash is needed later to move back to equities.

2. Be conservative: Buy stocks based on value and not based on momentum. Reduce your new purchases and take profits especially on momentum stocks. I buy one stock for every two or three stocks I sold during this stage.

3. Protect your portfolio with stop orders. It is one of the few times I recommend stop orders. If you watch the market every day, just place market orders when your stock falls to a specific price.

4. Buy contra ETFs for aggressive investors.

5. Sell cover calls. I prefer to sell the stocks I own.

6. Older folks may not want to sell the stocks with huge gains (due to tax consideration) or stocks that give them an income stream of dividends. They can use options to protect potential losses for the stocks they own.

What to do after the plunge

In the first year after the start of the plunge, do not start to buy unless they are very good values. Aggressive investors should start closing their short positions/put options and selling contra ETFs.

When the market plunges, it usually takes at least one year to recover as investors believe they have to sell to protect their remaining nest eggs. Those sectors that cause the bubble will take even longer to recover.

After the plunge, watch out for the interest rate. If it is still high, it is the best time to buy high-yield bonds (i.e., junk bonds). Ensure that the corporation issuing the bonds would not bankrupt; the bonds from the old GM in 2007 lost most of their values. They will appreciate when the interest rate drops that the government would routinely do to stimulate the economy. 2008 is not a good year to invest in stocks and bonds except the contra ETFs and selling shorts, but 2009 definitely is (it is my Early Recovery phase of the market cycle).

Personally, I prefer not to buy any stocks until the chart tells us to reenter the market. It is the fear that investors do not want to reenter the market. The market will always recover as in the past.

Even before the recovery, some sectors (called consumer staple) are doing better such as health care, foodstuff, utilities and pharmaceuticals that are always in demand. Interest-sensitive sectors such as housing and auto will suffer disproportionately. They are also called cyclical stocks. Consumer Discretionary are sectors that suffer a lot in a recession such as high-tech products.

What to do in early recovery and after

When the market is starting to recover (2003 and 2009 in the last two market cycles), the potential profit is the highest. Buy deeply-valued stocks on companies that have been beaten down. They will recover with the highest appreciation potential. I call it the bottom fishing strategy.

Larger companies are fishing too to acquire smaller companies that fit into their corporate synergy or small companies with the technology and/or the customer base they need.

Valued stocks could be defined a little differently in this phase. Many times P/E is not a good metric as most companies are losing money. 2003 is such a year. If you expect the recession to end in 2 years and the company has enough cash to survive in two years based on its annual burn rate, then it would be a buy candidate.

In both 2003 and 2009, I spotted at least one company that was acquired by a larger company. From my memory, one company in 2003 was acquired by IBM giving me more than 2 times return. In 2009, at least three companies were acquired giving me an average annualized return of over 200%.

Momentum strategy rewards us best from the end of the early recovery phase to the peak phase. The up phase started in 2004 for the 2000 market cycle and 2010 in the 2007 market cycle.

Note. The parameters of SMA-200, SMA-350, SMA-90, etc. and RSI are different for market exit/reentry, correction exit and individual stocks. These are the guidelines only. Stocks are more volatile than the market and are very different among them. Hence, define the 'days' according to the historical pattern of the individual stock and how often you trade them.

Filler: My translation from my Chinese friend's poem

When you understand "everything is changing", you won't be boosting your achievements. Today's splendid life could be a mess tomorrow.

When you understand "everything is changing", you won't be sad. Today's gloom could turn into sunshine tomorrow.

When you understand "everything is changing", you know today's gain could be tomorrow's loss and vice versa.

When you understand "everything is changing", there is no need to react to today's loss, gain, happiness and sadness.

Link: Making money during a crash.
https://www.youtube.com/watch?v=DjDCg4750dw

Sectors for market stages:
https://www.youtube.com/watch?v=FRdeXgf0rN8

3   Profitable Early Recovery

I had an 80% return in 2009 in my largest taxable account. I did not include it in my other books before as I just found the statement. Early Recovery, a phase of the market cycle defined by me, is the best time to make a profit. My chart told me to start to move to equity in September, 2009. I did in March, 2009 for other reasons. It could be luck, technique or both.

I did dip into the credit line of my equity loan (not recommended to most) due to lower interest rates than a margin interest. I paid back the loan right after I sold some stocks. The turnaround was high until I exhausted my short-term losses (tax loss harvest). The strategy is bottom fishing. Some sectors described are better in this stage of the market cycle.

I had similar success in 2003. I did not have a defined bottom fishing technique at that time. I expected the market to fully recover in two years. From Value Line, I selected stocks with high "Projected 3-5 year returns" and the short-term assets can last for two more years (judged by the burnt rates).

As the stocks are recovering earnings (E), the trailing P/E may not be a good indicator, but the Forward P/E may be. Most sites on evaluating stocks such as Fidelity have a value grade. Also look for candidates for acquisition. From the last recoveries, I spotted at least one such candidate. They are usually small companies (50 to 300M market cap) and have valuable assets such as customer base and patents. Aggressive investors should buy stocks with the worst timing grades and this the only time to do so; these beaten-up stocks could be big winners.

An article stated that the entire company of an internet company can fit into the conference room of Exxon, and it had the same market cap as Exxon if my memory serves me right. In early April, 2000, I switched all my tech mutual funds in my annuity into traditional sectors (better to cash in hindsight) to avoid the crash.

4   A non-correlation of the market and business

The Business Cycle (same as the Economic Cycle) is supposed to lag the Market Cycle[1] by about 6 months as the stock market is a leading indicator of the economy. As of May of 2013, this has not occurred. The U.S. economy does not correlate to the stock market. It seldom happens. The market has recovered most of its losses from 2007-2008 and actually is making new heights.

The economy is still in a recession considering the high unemployment / under-employment and the poor GDP growth. The global economies are more interconnected than before, and our trade partners are also not doing well. Though there have been some recent signs of recovery in the U.S. economy, the job employment may never reach its previous peak. As of 3/2016, the non-correlation continues.

Is this non-correlation important to us, the retail investors?

For an economist, the Economic Cycle is important. For an investor, the Market Cycle is important. Economists forecast business growth, GDP growth, job growth, housing start, etc., and plan accordingly. Investors care about the potential appreciation of their portfolios.

It could be the beginning of this non-correlation for the coming decade. There is a good chance economists can no longer depend on the previous correlation to use the market to predict the economy at least for a while. As long as the market is moving up, investors are not concerned with the non-correlation.

However, most likely the market will correlate again in the future with the economy as there has always been a correlation as far as I can remember. Until the following reasons of this non-correlation change, the correlation will continue.

The reasons for this non-correlation
1. Most big companies are now global companies.
    Hiring at these multinational corporations (MNCs) depends on where the offer is for the greatest benefits including low workforce salary, educated workers, tax credits, less taxes, stable government, good infrastructure, etc. A good portion of

MNCs' incomes are from foreign countries. Hence the U.S. market is getting less correlated with the U.S. economy which uses local employment as a measurement.

2. Too many government interventions.
   The government bailed out too many companies that should fail. No companies are too big to fail. It has not punished the executives/bankers to get us into this recession thru their greed. The market may falsely expect that future failing companies will be bailed out. Hence, the stock market is expected to be protected by the government.

3. There is still a lot of easy money.
   Since the recession, banks are flooded with government money to invest. They loan out money to investors instead of loaning it to small businesses and house buyers to stimulate the economy. In addition, the demands from businesses and potential house buyers have been reduced. The cash reserves if not loaned out must be very high.
   Corporations now have the highest cash reserves for a long while. They use their cash reserves to buy back their own stocks, acquire companies and increase dividends. All these actions increase their stock values. Dividend stocks are flocked by income seekers especially with low bond yields.
   When the government borrows a lot of money (to the ceiling literally), everything including the market looks good. However, somehow and sometimes the taxpayers will pay for those debts to China, Japan and whatever other treasury buyers. Today the U.S. has a benefit: It will repay the debtors with depreciated dollars (not true if 2016). A country loses its competitive edge if a good percentage of the GDP is used for servicing those debts. If the USA were a company that could not service its debts, it would be bankrupt. Most believe this is the primary reason.

4. Government regulations typically do not help the economy. To illustrate, the expected Obamacare is discouraging small businesses from hiring.

5. Today's market may not be a good indicator of its value, if this were considered to be a commodity unit (a combination of natural resources including gold) instead of the USD.

6. There are too many factors that influence both the market and the economy in separate directions. Examples include the recent

shale energy discovery which could improve the economy. A new war would do the opposite.

What should be done

1. The government cannot pump that much cash into the economy.

   Depreciating our currency is a short-term solution at best as it would improve our trade both ways. The status of being a reserve currency is shaken.
2. The United States government must address how to service its debt! The high debt will deteriorate the United States' competitive edge in the global markets. A high percentage of our GDP to service the debts will not help the economy.
3. We and the government need to bite the bullet with more taxes, more incentives to create jobs, less entitlements, less welfare... Ending the current two wars and avoiding future wars are almost mandatory to improve the economy.
4. The U.S. economy cannot be recovered without job recovery. The money spent in creating jobs will be better spent than on welfare and unemployment benefits. Hiring more government employees is the problem, not a solution.

Conclusion

It may be better to invest in a rising market than holding the depreciating cash. However, this non-correlation will not continue forever. The basic reason that stock appreciates is the company's ability to improve its earning. P/E is still the best yardstick on how fairly a company stock is priced. With a fixed 'E' for example and a rising 'P', the company's stock will be overpriced and will return to its average value (the average P/E for the last five years). The correlation will be back again in a matter of time.

Footnote

[1]The market can only act as a leading indicator or proxy of economic activity if there is consensus on the direction. Sometimes what is coming in six months is fairly predictable but at other times when pundits are at odds the future course is fuzzy. So, market indices are really tracking where consensus "thinks" GDP is going'.

To be clear a market index is a summary of where consensus

believes the economy is headed and this sentiment is a proxy for forward earnings. For the playing stocks and not the index, it is their cumulative sentiment which acts as a guide.

Afterthoughts
- There are many other correlations. The following should correlate with the economy: construction industry, employment, commodity /commodity-related currency and oil. Once a while and for a good reason, they do not.
- QE, printing money, foreign loans (to China...), reserve currency, debt ceiling all mean the same: Live in a higher standard of living than we can afford.
  When Uncle Sam unsuccessfully uses all the tools to maintain our living standard and being the world's policeman, he runs out of tools. That will build a higher cliff for us to fall.
  Hopefully, shale energy will save our economy.
- The global economy still has not recovered as of July, 2013 according to this article.
  (http://www.telegraph.co.uk/finance/economics/10174862/Renewed-fear-of-global-recession-as-companies-rein-in-spending-plans.html)
- Here are some economic indicators.
  http://en.wikipedia.org/wiki/Economic_indicator
- This time is REALLY different. Your Dad's generation does not have the internet, powerful PC, low-interest commission, trading at a click of the mouse... Global economies are better connected via the internet, shipping... All these affect our lives and economies.

5   A tale of two market plunges

I gather the data of the last two plunges (2000 and 2007) and check out what they have in common.

All the data are for information and education purposes only and so are the conclusions. All market plunges are different but some common characteristics do exist. Market plunges older than 2000 may not be useful as the market conditions then were very different from today's market.

Charts

The first one is for 2007 and the next one for 2000.

The following charts are also saved in the following link in case you read this book on a small screen. Type the following link in your browser to display the graph on your PC if desirable.

http://ebmyth.blogspot.com/2013/07/chart-market-plunge-2007.html

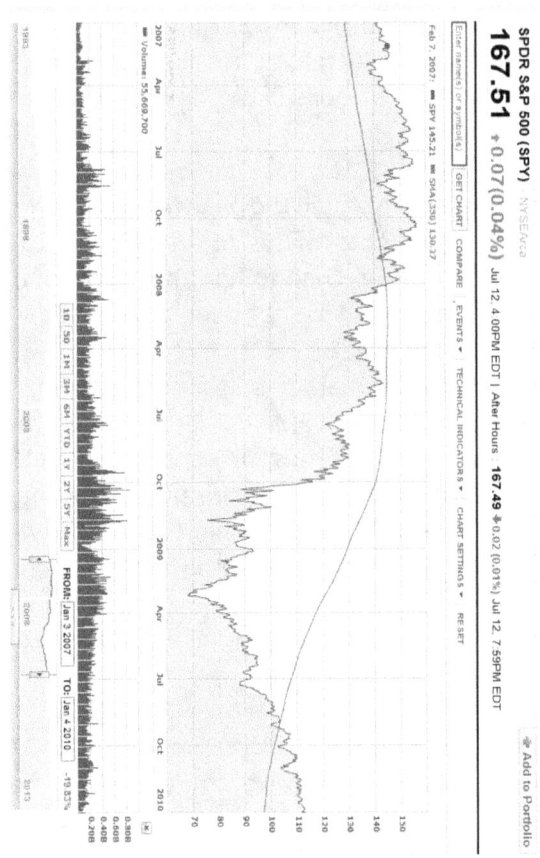

2007 Market Plunge Chart from Yahoo!Finance

Explanations:
- The red line is the 350-day SMA (simple moving average for the last 350 trade sessions). Sell when the price is below the SMA

and buy when it is above the SMA. It gives us the exit point from the market and the reentry point to the market

.

- This chart uses SPY, an ETF simulating the S&P 500 index. A total market ETF would be a better choice unless you only trade the S&P 500 stocks. If most of your stocks are in small caps, use an index ETF for small caps. Instead of using an ETF, you can use any market index.

- The exit point is Jan. 7, 2008 (a brief indicator in Nov., 2007). Either exit point is fine. We should start to exit the market on Nov. 26, 2007 and this market plunge was nice to give us one more exit point. In reality, it takes us more time to exit the market totally. It looks like a double peak to me in technical terms.

- It is not possible to catch the peak from the chart (July – October, 2007), but this chart helps us to prevent further and bigger losses. I have researched to find the common metrics for peaks and bottoms. They have not been proven so far in my tests.

- The return to the market is around September, 2009 from the chart (above the 350 SMA). I returned to stocks in February, 2009, right at the bottom. It is just pure luck, my timing was based on the duration after the plunge, or many other factors that I may have forgotten. That's one reason we should take notes and learn from our experiences.

- Enlarge the chart by selecting a shorter date range or using a larger screen.

The following graph displays the same for the 2000 market plunge. If you have a problem in viewing it on the small screen, display it on your PC screen via the same link above. It is better to produce it yourself using Yahoo!Finance or one of the many sites to produce SMA charts.

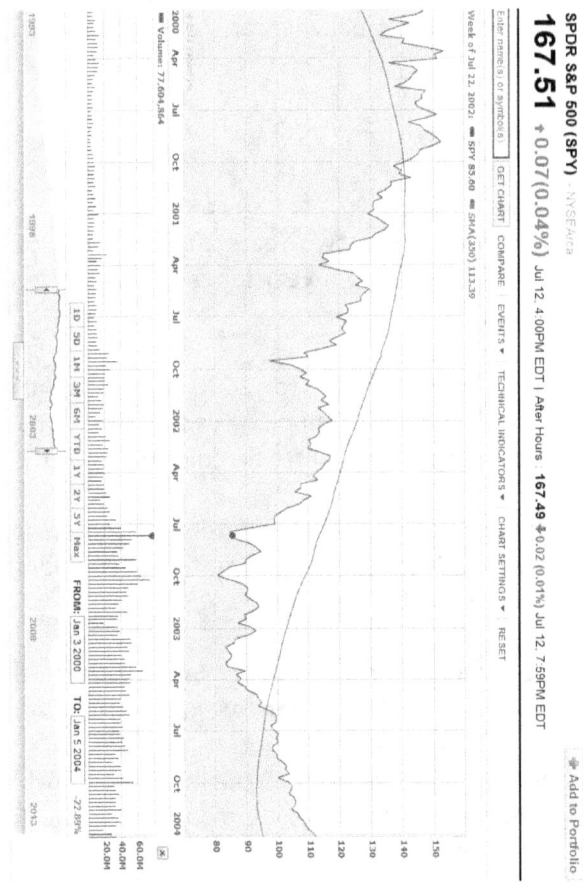

2000 Market Plunge Chart from Yahoo!Finance

Significant Periods

All the durations are estimates. They are different in each market plunge.

- Plunging period.
  It is the period between the start of the plunge (i.e., the peak) and the bottom. On the average, the duration of the plunge is about a year. Do not buy stocks during this period except selling shorts and buying contra ETFs to the market for aggressive investors.

- Early Recovery.

It is the period between the market bottom and the mid part of the recovery and usually it starts one and a half year after the plunge.

Detecting the bottom

1. By the duration.
   It is about one to two years after the start of the plunge. It takes at least half a year longer for the offending sector(s) to recover.

   The offending sector for 2000 (the sector that caused the plunge) was the technology sector. The housing sector and the finance sector were the culprits in 2007.

   Some of the stocks in the offending sectors lose most or all of their values such as many internet companies in 2000 and Lehman Brothers in 2007.

   The market recovered faster in 2007 than 2000 due to the government intervention by excessively printing money.

2. By the total loss.
   Another hint is how much the market has lost from the peak. From the next table, 45% is a good bet. I start buying on 40% loss instead of 45%. There are many great bargains and we do not want to miss the opportunities.

3. By the 350-day SMA.
   For more conservative investors, wait for the stock price to pass the 350-day SMA (or other SMA such as the 200-day SMA). The 'day' is the last trade session.

All the market stages can seldom be predicted precisely. We are responsible for our own actions. Your actions also depend on your risk tolerance. A conservative investor would leave the market entirely on the first hint and return to the market slowly and gradually after the first hint.

Offending Sectors

Usually the offending sectors (the sectors that cause the bubble to burst) take at least 2 years to recover. Try out the SMA-350 and SMA-200 charts on the ETFs of these offending sectors.

ETFs and more articles on the offending sectors:

2007:   Housing ETF XHB and Financial ETF XLF.
        Housing bubble.
(http://en.wikipedia.org/wiki/United_States_housing_bubble)

        .

2000:   Technology ETF XLK and Telecommunication IYZ.
        Internet bubble.
(http://en.wikipedia.org/wiki/Dot-com_bubble)

Depending on which report you read, the dates will not be exact. Some claim the housing crisis started in 2008 instead of 2007 and the internet crisis started in 2001 instead of 2000.

Summary by tables

Again, the dates are not exact and they depend on an individual interpretation. My table indicates 51% average loss and I use 45% as a more conservative number. I use my own dates and interpretations on the following tables.

Table: Market Plunges

Market Plunge	Months (Peak to Bottom)	Loss	Annualized loss
2000	17	56%	40%
2007	25	47%	23%
Average	21	51%	31%

Table: Vital Dates

Market Plunge	Peak	Bottom	Indicator Exit	Indicator Reenter
2000	08/28/00	09/20/02	10/30/00	05/26/03
2007	10/12/07	03/06/09	01/03/08	09/08/09

Most investors were fully invested in 2007 and 2008 and NOT fully invested in 2009. If you followed the exit indicator and reenter indicator, you should do far better than the average investor.

Afterthoughts

- Many including myself do not believe a market plunge is coming as of 7/2014. However, we have to be careful with the following analysis. Run the simple chart to spot any indication of a market plunge at least once a month. The following are from my experiences.

  o Among my top-performing screens for the last 3 months, many top-performing screens are from the peak stage (defined by me) rather than other stages in a market cycle.

  o The typical market cycle is about 5 years. We have about 6 years since 2007.

  o The stock market has not reached the bubble stage yet. It will if it continues to rise at this pace in 2014.

- On 6/20/2013, the market lost more than 2% in a day due to the Fed indicating no more easy money. The bond yield jumped. The Fed has been dumping about 1 trillion a year. When the money stops, the market would crash and the 2% loss seems to be a canary. Hopefully the current correction would be less than 10%

  [Update: only 6%]. Wall Street depends on the government handouts and the government is running out of tools to fix the economy.

- Some REITs are inversely affected by the rising interest rate. http://seekingalpha.com/article/1570772-american-capital-mortgage-investment-was-the-baby-thrown-out-with-the-bathwater

- Will the market go even higher as of 6/2014? We have to compare the risk / reward ratio. If the risk is too high, we may want to take some chips off the table.

- To me, there are 4 groups of investors.
  1. Institutional investors. Their performances vary. In short, hedge funds as a group have not beaten the market in the last 5 years.

2. Mutual funds. Most cannot do market timing from their own regulations and as a group they do not beat the market after expenses.
3. Retail investors are always on the wrong side of the market via fear and greed.
4. While investors from #1 to #3 are losers, there must be some winners beating the market as a trade is a zero-sum game. In theory, we cannot beat the mutual fund managers who have better resources. However, we can use market timing to our advantage.

#Fillers
"Hold" rating from analysts means "Sell as fast as you can". Very seldom, there is a "Sell".

Filler: The 0.5%
The world has been controlled by 0.5% who are the wealthiest and make the rules of the world. These folks own US businesses and EU businesses, and they make money in every way and everywhere they see opportunities. The following link and Tesla's mega factory in China forced me to think; it is a case of Biden vs the 0.5%.
https://finance.yahoo.com/news/citigroup-hire-1-700-people-093000440.html

6   Secular bull market is coming!

My definitions

A secular stock market is a prolonged period (about 12 to 22 years) that the market is heading in one particular direction. There have been secular bear markets and secular bull markets depending on the direction of the stock market.

Market cycles exist within a secular market. Market cycles last for about 5 years. The market cycle of 2000-2007 lasted for about 7 years and the current one from 2007-to now (2016) for about 8 years so far.

Within a year there are usually two mini market cycles (I call them 5% corrections or dips/surges and sometimes one 5% and one 5-15% correction). The surges provide the best time to sell stocks and the dips provide the best time to buy stocks if there is no market plunge.

The secular market cycle, market cycle and yearly corrections (also defined by me as mini market cycles) are not scientific concepts. Hence, their average durations are very rough estimates. I use 20 years for the secular market cycle for the ease to memorize while 15 could be a better average.

Market Cycle vs. Economic Cycle

Understanding the Market Cycle is important to investors and the Economic Cycle (also known as the Business Cycle) is important to economists and businessmen. Do not be confused with the two. The secular economic cycle usually follows the secular market cycle as indicated in the last 60 years. With the obvious exception of the current one (2007-2016), the economic cycle usually lags the market cycle by an average of 6 months.

My prediction: The secular bull will start in 2018

Whenever a famous person predicts with any certainty that the end of the world is coming or the Dow will double next year, it is loudly broadcasted over the news. I predict that the next secular bull market will start as early as in 2018. Who would take me, a nobody, and his prediction seriously? If it does not happen, check out which ones of my many arguments are wrong and/or any unpredictable event or events have happened.

This is a bold prediction! There are reasons why it might happen and also reasons why it might not happen. I could write a book on this topic but I will spare you the details. However, let us carefully scrutinize the coming events to better clarify my prediction.

Timing is everything even though there is nothing truly considered as perfect timing. But be aware that reacting too early to a secular bull market can cost you money, and reacting too late to a secular bull market can miss the profit opportunity. Vice versa for a secular bear market.

Past secular markets

If the market is good, the economy would be good and every person would have a job in theory. Even the poor would benefit from the more generous government benefits and the increased individual generosity. Today, global corporations can hire any worker in any place in the world at the least cost to change the US employment picture.

I have identified the last three secular bull and bear markets (again they are rough estimates):
   Secular bear market: 1960-1980
   Secular bull market: 1980-2000
   Secular bear market: 2000-2020

I did not include secular markets before 1960 as these times did not resemble today's market conditions.

In a secular bull market, every investor is a genius. Most of our stocks rise with the tide in a bull market. With the profits from the market, we spend more on disposable consumer products. During wars, most sectors fall except those making bombs, jets and tanks.

The cause of secular markets: War or lack of war
What causes the secular markets that usually last for about 20 years? My contribution to this theory is that war is the major

common denominator to the secular bear markets. Though I have not read any article that distinguishes it out, I am sure the concept is so obvious that someone would have reached the same conclusion.

In the 1960s, it was the Vietnam War and the effects after this war. Today it is the two wars in the Middle East. Wars cost us a lot of resources. When these resources are devoted to the economy after the wars, the economy would grow.

After each major war, our leaders do not forget the harmful effects at least for a while. They cannot get re-elected with a new war, so there will be no major war for a long while. That's my explanation of the secular bull market from 1980-2000. After the year 2000, our leaders forgot the harmful effects of wars and history repeated itself.

Wars are the primary cause of a secular bear market and bubbles are the triggers to market plunges. Usually, recessions follow market plunges. In 2000, we had the internet bubble and in 2007 we had the housing bubble. With minor exceptions, all bubbles are caused by excessive valuation and they will come back to the average value eventually.

In 2000, many internet companies had no profits or their P/Es were very high (some over 40) from the average P/E of about 15. In 2007, the market housing value was too high due to the availability of easy credit. The only exception of the bubbles is the recent price of gold which does not really appreciate that much but the dollar depreciates. The two wars partly contributed to its appreciation.

If the government concentrates its efforts on the economy rather than wars, it could detect the bubble earlier before its burst and at least the economy would have had a soft landing rather than the hard landing in 2008. Remind the politicians to avoid any future war and use your voting power to enforce it.

We should have learned from the French before we participated in the Vietnam War or the Russians before we did the same in Afghanistan. We have been dragged many times by Israel to the Middle East wars but we have no business there.

We cannot afford to be the global policeman. Our youth should enjoy the best time of their lives in colleges or new jobs instead of being sent to the front line. The National Guard should guard in case of emergency and natural disasters, not to be sent to the front line.

I expect we'll have a prolonged bull market as early as in 2018 after ending the two wars completely; still there is no sign it will end soon as of 3/2016. By 2015 and hopefully earlier, the housing problem should be resolved by absorbing the inventory and the Euro crisis should also be resolved (as of 3/2016, it is not). The politicians will not forget the harmful effects from the wars, the secular bull market will hopefully continue for the next 15 to 20 years.

War and the lack of war determines the secular market to me. However, there are many other factors playing an important role. In 1974, the oil crisis made the secular bear market even worse.

Secular bull market could be postponed to 2020

The following events may prevent a secular bull market from starting in 2018 and postpone it to 2020 and hopefully earlier:

1. A possible war with China due to protecting Taiwan from invasion.

   When the Chinese government cannot suppress the internal unrest and to detract attention from its own inability, it would force itself to invade Taiwan. More likely, a trade blockage by China would be more effective with the tight economic ties between each other.

2. Another probable cause for a war is the U.S. military backing of Japan and other Asian countries on the disputes of the islands near Japan or the Philippines.

   It is illogical to borrow more money from China to contain China.

3. World climate change adversely affects the food supply. If technology has not improved the production of food in the last 50 years, there would be a famine in poor countries today.

   Global warming leads to many problems such as the shortage of drinking water. India would suffer most when China, the owner of the water source in Tibet, would redirect the water flow for its own citizens.

4. Natural disasters such as earthquakes and hurricanes. California is long overdue for a big one. Japan suffered its worst Tsunami in recent history.

5. Huge budget deficit.

   If the government continues to spend at the current rate, the prolonged unbalanced budget could never get us out of the recession. In addition, the government's excessive obligations on generous welfare, social security, Medicare and other entitlement budgetary obligations are growing too quickly and lead to imminent bankruptcy. We would already be bankrupt if the US government were a company.

   The Fiscal Cliff has not really been fixed and we are still too deep into debts. We cannot pass our debt obligations onto the next generation forever.

6. The trapped gas and oil could provide us with enough energy for the next 50 years. The successful extraction could accelerate the start of the secular bull market one year earlier. We're facing oil dumping by oil-producing countries as of 2015.

Conclusion

Be realistic, check out these developments and adjust such predictions accordingly. An accurate prediction based on current events would better assess the risk of the market.

I do not suggest staying away from the market until 2018. As before, there will be market cycles within a secular market and yearly corrections. When we are in a secular bull market, we should be more aggressive, and vice versa in a secular bear market.

Statistically, there are three recessions in a secular bear market. Is it coincidental? As of January of 2014, there were two so far.

Is 2009 to 2016 a secular bull market? No, the bull market has to be correlated with the economy and the economy has not been fully recovered as of 2016. This exception is due to the excessive money supply. The money has to be paid back. Before we have our debts under control and balance our budget, our economy has not been recovered.

Afterthoughts

- I predicted a market top on April, 2012 within days.

- Signs of an economy recovery:

  1. Increase corporate profits.
  2. Increase employment.
  3. Increase housing starts.
  4. Decrease Federal deficit.
  5. Increase the growth of GDP.
  6. Rising values in some sectors such as consumers, high tech., housing, etc.

  As of 1/2014, #2 and #3 seem to be improving. #1 is OK. However #4 is not.

  When you borrow money (#4) and use it productively, you can improve #1 to #3. I have strong doubts about this economic recovery.

  We're having a non-correlation in the Economy and the market.

The following information is supplied by my friend Norman.

- Traditional theory would say a 20-years secular cycle with 10 years between the major pullbacks. The first major pullback was called the Capital Crisis (1997-2003). The second major pullback was called the Real Estate Crisis (2007-2009). According to this theory, the next major pullback will be 2017 (Capital Crisis).

- In between major crises are business cycle pullbacks (Kitchen Cycle) approximately 5 years each. These are also called inventory cycles.

  It should be noted that these have always existed, even before Capitalism in 1720. During the secular bull market, they are muted by the positive market trend. However, they still exist.

- Norman believes we have started the secular bull market on Jan. 1, 2013. The secular 20-year cycle is based on the generations. The X generation has just moved into old age and the millennials are becoming mid-life consumers--This is a huge generation, similar to the Baby Boomers and demand for everything is going up.

- Nikolai Kondratiev would say the generational economic cycle has 4 seasons. He said it lasted 50-60 years. http://en.wikipedia.org/wiki/Nikolai_Kondratiev

7   Market prediction for a new year

This article demonstrates how I predict the market to be. It is for 2013, but the logic is valid for predictions about the future market.

In the article "My prediction for 2013 – all other predictions will be wrong", Larry Smith, a respected contributor at Seeking Alpha, suggested that many yearly predictions on 2012 by known organizations and famed individuals are often wrong.

Larry said,

"To prove my point, I thought I would look at some of the 2012 market forecasts that were made at the end of 2011. Let's start by looking at some of the S&P 500 forecasts that were made by the leading Wall Street firms. **Morgan Stanley** (MS) takes the worst prediction prize by forecasting an end-of-year the S&P 500 closing price of 1167, off by almost 300 points. **Goldman Sachs** (GS) predicted 1250 as the closing price of the S&P 500 price and **Seabreeze Partners** misfired on the high end by forecasting the S&P 500 closing price of 1527. Click here to see all the major brokerage firms' predictions for 2012. Most of the firms underestimated the size of the stock market rise.

Individual forecasters were not any better; here are some quotes from relatively well-known investors."

I agree with him completely, but there are exceptions and I try to be one of them. We can profit a lot from an accurate prediction. We need a prediction to be a framework on how we want to invest for the year and adjust the prediction as events surface.

My past prediction
Why should you want to follow a prediction from a nobody like me? My predictions have been on track many times, particularly for the year 2000, 2003 and 2009. In 2012, SPY (similar to the S&P 500 index) had a return of 13%. My prediction is 10%, off by 3%.

2013 is harder to predict and it depends on whether we have a QEn and the interest rates that have no way to go but up. We've been up too much since 2009 and the economy is still off with poor employment rates.

8   What to do in mid-year

The following may work or may not work in the future. It could fit into a data-fitting category. I include it here and will update whether it works in the coming years. From my observation, when the market over-reacts in the first half of the year, it will usually (but not all the time) correct itself in the second half of the year.

There are two camps on what you should do in mid-year.

1. If the market has moved far more than its predicted share (such as double the predicted return), act opposite for the rest of the year. I belong to this camp.
2. Flow with the market's momentum.

Basically, they are opposite of each other. Portfolios need constant manipulations as my mid-year action adjustment for 2012. It depends on a good prediction at the beginning of the year. I did not adjust mine in 2012, but it might provide valuable lessons. The rear mirror is always clearer.

2012 as an example

I predicted 10% for 2012. SPY was about 13%, so it is quite good.

At mid-year, we calculate how much it will still go up by the formula (predicted percent – actual YTD percent).

As of July, 2012, the SPY's return is 7% YTD, and it is better than expected. From the above formula (10% - 7%), we should still have 3% gain to go. Hence, we do not change our investment in stocks. In reality, it gained another 6% from July to the end of 2012, so the action is correct.

Inconclusive conclusion

To conclude, if the market has substantially gained its share of the predicted return, it is time to be conservative. Be more aggressive when the first half of the year loses more than its predicted return. It is a very rough and inconclusive guideline and I will test it out more in the future.

In any case, in mid-year we should make some adjustments such as balancing the sectors, monitor the risk of a market plunge and detect yearly dips especially if there is no dip so far.

Again, it is just a prediction and hopefully we have more rights than wrongs in the long run.

9   The worst scenario

From the described hints, you move all your stocks to cash but the market may keep on climbing and making new heights. You would be frustrated on how much you would have gained and hence move back to stocks. Then the market plunges. It is the worst in market timing. My suggestion:

- In the first hint of a market plunge, move a percentage of your stocks (preferably the risky stocks first) to cash. The percentage depends on your personal risk tolerance.

- Gradually move more to cash when the market is still climbing. If I expect the market to move up 2% more, I place sell orders at 2% more than the market prices.

- When the market plunges or the hints are all indicative of a market plunge, sell all. Personally, my 'sell all' is about 50% of my portfolio. It is not because I do not trust my strategy, but I do not bet all in either direction. That is just me.

No one can tell you what to do as everyone's situation is different. If you depend on your investments for daily income, be more conservative.

The most conservative investor can stay close to 100% in cash during the entire peak stage of the market cycle and invest in long-term bond funds when the interest rates are high. He has to ignore the excitement in the market. He only buys stocks at the bottom. I bet he is doing better than most retail investors with the least risk.

This scenario may not happen as our charts also tell us to return to the market – we call it a false signal.

10   Market timing from 2008 to 2015

Produce the SMA-350 chart using any chart system. This time I switched to my Fidelity broker as I cannot produce the same chart with the new version of Yahoo!Finance. It could be my fault.

Specify SPY, an ETF to simulate the market, SMA (Simple Moving Average), 350 sessions and the period from Dec. 1, 2008 to Dec. 1, 2015. The following are my findings.

- In my previous chart from 2000 to 2009, we only had one false signal. False signals tell us to exit the market but tell us to reenter the market shortly. In most cases, it does not change much in our portfolio except some tax consequences for taxable accounts.
- Between 2010 and 2015, we had several false signals. It tells us the market is more volatile than the period from 2000 to 2010. There could be too many followers on this technical indicator.
- I could reduce this number of false signals by using SMA-400 (400 sessions instead of 350). I do not as I predict 2016 could be more dangerous with possible interest rate hikes. "SMA-350" alarms us earlier than "SMA-400".
- Again, market timing is not a science. It is only a prediction. It has been proven from 2000 to 2010, but I do not expect it will always work. Otherwise, we will have poor folks.
- I had about 50% in cash before the August, 2015 correction. If I followed the chart, I should have 100% in cash. I could not conquer my greed.
- Even today (12/1/2015) when the stock price of SPY is above the SMA-350, I still want to have about 50% in cash as the market is risky to me.

I will have less cash after I buy stocks using my year-end loser strategy. You have to decide the percentage of cash you want to hold based on your risk tolerance. The less risk tolerance you have, the higher is the percentage of cash you want to hold.

Section III: Correction

1   Correction

Market timing has been judged wrongly by many. Just check out how the two major plunges can be detected easily by my simple chart.

Corrections are harder to detect. So far, I have more rights than wrongs in detecting corrections.

Everyone has its own definition of a correction and mine is as follows. A correction is a 10% or more down from the peak of the last 180 days or more than 5% down in a month. Sometimes, corrections continue to 20% loss. My definition of a market plunge is the loss of 40% or more from the recent peak to the bottom. There is a gray area between a 20% to 40% loss.

From my definition, there is no correction in 2013 and that is quite rare. On the average it happens at least once every year since 2000 depending on my interpretation. I also estimate two minor corrections of 5% every year if we do not have a 10% correction.

Corrections provide us opportunities to enter the market. Temporary peaks provide us opportunities to sell. They happen about one to two times a year on the average but their frequencies fluctuate widely. I usually start selling at the expected peaks, and buying at the expected bottoms. Your cash position depends on your risk tolerance. 'Buy-and-hold' investors can just ignore corrections and this chapter.

Some hints (not always reliable) predict the temporary market peak:

- Up more than 10% of the expected gain. To illustrate, you predicted this year's total return is 12% in the beginning of the year. In March, the market has already gained 12%, there is a good chance it is close to the yearly peak and you should act accordingly. Review the stocks you own and sell those with less appreciation potential first.
- The market has exceeded a good percent over the last peak. Define this percent based on your risk tolerance.

- Compare the annualized market P/E (SPY or any market index ETF) to its 5-year average (10-year average is fine too).
- Foreign markets are down and ours are up by a good margin.
- The interest rate. When it rises, the market will be down.
- It happens more than three consecutive days that there are more stocks advancing than retreating.
- It happens more than three consecutive days that the number of new highs is more than the number of new lows.
- From Finviz.com, SPY's SMA200 exceeds 10% (= (Price − SMA)/SMA). SMA-200 is Single Moving Average for the last 200 sessions. It indicates it may be temporarily peaking. Use it for reference only as it is not always reliable.
- From Finviz.com, SPY's RSI(14), the relative strength index based on the last 14 days, exceeds 55%. It indicates that it may be overbought. This is for reference only as it is not always reliable.
- There are always reasons for corrections such as the market is overvalued, rising interest rates, degrading corporation earnings and trade wars.

Conclusion

Corrections are harder to detect compared to the market plunges which we have excellent results so far from 2000.

Do not bet the entire farm on corrections especially when the market is risky. Keep less than 25% of your portfolio in cash on the expected peaks.

When the market corrects, it is a buying opportunity. However, when the market starts to plunge, we should exit the market as the losses could be high. If all the conditions in the following table are exceeded, most likely the market is peaking. One's opinion.

SMA-50%	SMA-200%	SMA-350%	Avg. of the 3 the SMA%	RSI(14)
4%	6%	11%	9%	65%

2   Six signs of a correction

Six signs of a correction:

1. All my technical indicators show the market is peaking and overbought. SPY is an ETF simulating the market of the S&P 500 stocks. As of 6/29/2014, the RSI(14) is at 67% and the SMA-200% is at 8.35%. SMA-200% measures how far away the stock price is from its simple moving average of the last 200 trade sessions.

    You may argue that you do not believe in technical analysis. However, many institutional fund managers learn technical analysis and they will act accordingly. It is one of the many tools that hedge fund managers use to 'hedge'. Most mutual fund managers cannot practice market timing bound by the rules and regulations.

2. Newton's Law of Gravity has never been proven wrong (some humor to get your attention). What goes up must come down. The market has been up even after inflation. However, it takes a breather from time to time. A small one is called a correction and a big one is called a market plunge.
3. We did not have one such correction of 10% in 2013, so the time is ripe. The average is about one correction of 10% or more and about 1.5 corrections for 5% in a year. Many experts predicted wrongly on a correction in 2013. I do not bet against them to be wrong two times in a row.
4. There are more articles predicting a correction than articles arguing against it. It could be a self-fulfilling prophecy. It is the herd mentality. One's opinion.
5. The market has low volumes and narrow ranges for many days may indicate that the market is changing direction. The sea is calmest before a storm.
6. I am not convinced that I can make a lot of profit even if there is no correction. To me, the market is fully valued. It is my reward / risk ratio. I prefer not to make the last buck and have a good sleep.

How to protect yourself

It depends on your risk tolerance.

1. Accumulate cash from 0% to 50%. I recommend 15% for most. 0% is for those who ignore the signs. It was a great selection for 2013. I select 50% as I'm more conservative than most.
2. Place stop orders. Adjust them when they have appreciated in price. Some stocks are more volatile than others. I prefer to use stop orders in market plunges rather than corrections, as corrections are too brief to be effective.
3. Short the market. I do not recommend shorting in most cases. Buying a contra ETF may help. In any case, do not risk money you cannot afford to lose.
4. Use options to protect your portfolio.
5. Prepare a list of stocks to buy when there is a correction, and wait for a better time to invest.

Do not treat my (or all others') predictions as gospel. Predictions are just predictions. It is like buying insurance that we do not expect to collect from.

I have to admit market timing is not an exact science. Hopefully we are more right than wrong.

Summary of comments on the article

There are two camps: one who believes and one who does not believe. It is as expected. I will not take credit if there will be a correction within a month, or take the blame if there will be none in the next 3 months. From my record, I have more right than wrong predictions, but it may have nothing to do with future market predictions. Here is my summary:

1. I did think of other signs as mentioned by some of my readers: interest rate, oil price, current events... I expect interest rates will start rising by the end of the year. The recent rise in oil price is due to the turmoil in the Middle East. The current events including Ukraine and the Middle East seem not to be a factor as our leader does not want to participate in this.

2. I do not expect a market plunge (over 30% down) as I do not see any bubbles (those bubble stocks are too few). My prediction:

These bubble stocks will be half the peaks achieved in 2013 and 2014 by the end of 2014. To me, all stock trades are predictions. Some materialize and some do not.

3. Corrections are harder to detect than market plunges. After I detect a plunge, I will spend most of my time in protecting my portfolio.

3 Anticipating a correction

'Buy-and-hold' investors can ignore this chapter. This chapter enhances the last one.

You should try to sell as many stocks as you own before the correction comes and buy them back during and after the expected correction. It does not always work. However, it is good to churn your portfolio to ensure it has better appreciation potential at the expense of capital gain taxes in non-retirement accounts.

Signs of a market top (same as correction is coming)

- The market has been up for over 4 months from the last dip.
- The market has gained more than the predicted share.
- If most of your stocks are at the peak, take some profits.
- Use Technical Analysis (via use of charts) as below.

   Here is one of the charts that could predict temporary market dips and surges. Buy when the price is above the SMA (simple moving average) and sell when it is below. This example uses 50 days for SMA for 2012. SMA-50% is also available from Finviz.com.

   Vary the number of days and/or use other indicators to reduce noise or improve the trading frequency to fit your individual needs.

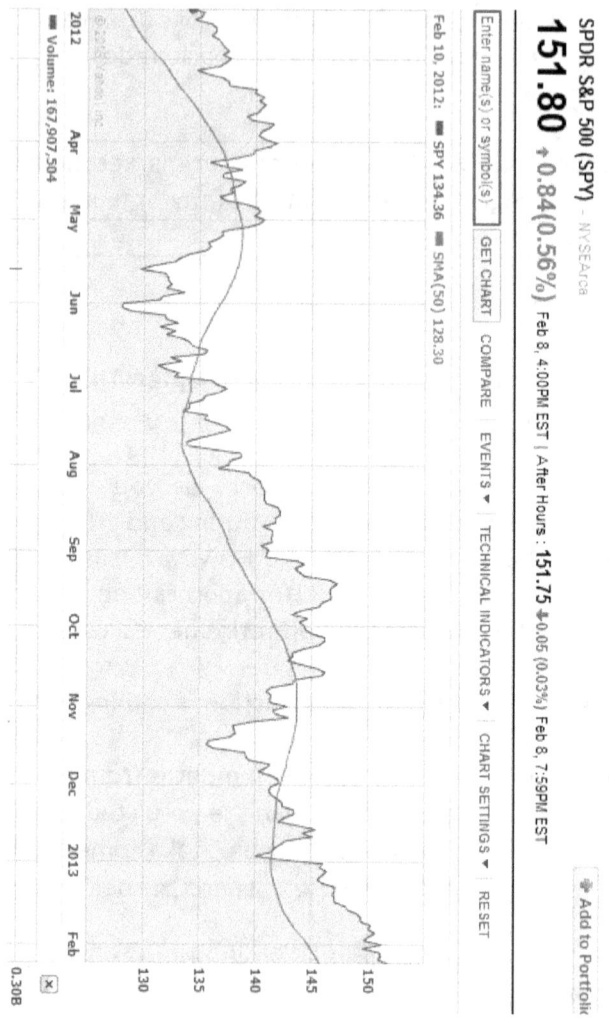

Source: Yahoo!Finance.

If you are reading this book on a small screen and cannot see the chart, type the following into your browser.
http://ebmyth.blogspot.com/2013/09/correction-example.html

There are too many trades in the above chart especially in the month of April. The period from July 1 to Oct. 15 is a good capture of the upward trend. It is useful but not perfect. Try to use SMA-100 instead of the above SMA-50.

Example of a market top

The following is from my blog written on May 19, 2011 and it turned out to be quite accurate. Check why I expected a correction would be coming. Hopefully we can spot the next one with similar reasoning. However, there is no guarantee for future performance and predictions.

Click here on the actual blog and the summary follows.
http://www.tonyp4idea.blogspot.com/2011/05/anticipating-correction.html

As of May 19, 2011, the market had been up by about 9% YTD. The experts were divided on whether the market would take a correction with convincing arguments for and against.

I had been selling stocks several weeks before and moved most of my Annuity positions to a money market fund. My total cash was 25% and I was still selling. I tried to sell most of my stocks at 5 to 10% higher than the market prices. Hence, even if there were no correction, I was still selling far better than my current prices and it was a reasonable insurance policy. I predicted that the market was risky at that time; you have to trust your prediction and act accordingly as it did.

After I had accumulated more than 30% in cash, I played the 'Buy one and Sell two' strategy betting I could spot stocks better than others. I tried to sell the stocks I bought right away for a small profit as I still expected a correction.

* Arguments for no correction:

- QE3 would materialize (even it will not amount to a lot of cash due to the debt ceiling).
- Corporate profits are still rising.
- The economy is improving.

* Arguments for correction:

- QE3 will not be materialized and no money will be used to stimulate the economy.
- The market is taking a breather after 9% YTD (I expect 5% rise in mid-year).
- Slim chance for the rule 'Stay away in May' as it had not been working for the two consecutive years except in today's extended bull market.
- There are financial problems from China, EU, Japan and N. Africa.
- With tightening margin requirements on commodities, oil..., speculative trades will be reduced (good for the long term).

The above is a summary of what the experts said. I did not do any research (as it is already available from the web). I summarized their opinions, selected what made sense to me, and acted accordingly.

I chose the middle road by not taking extreme actions such as selling all my holdings and heavily investing in contra ETFs.

Afterthoughts

- My Elastic Band Theory.
  The more you stretch an elastic band, the more it will rebound. When a stock's timing score is 10 (the best), it has no way to go but down. That is similar to the general market.

  The risk/reward ratio is too high as of 4/2013. Unless you have a time machine, you may not want to make the last buck.
- A related article from SA.
  (http://seekingalpha.com/article/1344071-5-reasons-why-i-am-shorting-the-market)

Links
Original blog:
http://www.tonyp4idea.blogspot.com/2011/05/anticipating-correction.html
An article on preparing for a correction.
http://www.forbes.com/sites/investor/2014/05/19/five-things-to-do-in-a-stock-market-correction/

#Filler: Roadblocks to progress

We use privacy to stop facial recognition. The device from Ring has reduced a lot of thefts and possibly crimes. Similar to stem cell research. That's why China is passing us in these areas.

4   Market correction example

I have 50% in cash before the August (2015) correction. I should have 100% if I followed my chart. However, we are just human beings blinded by our greed / fears and emotional attachment.

Stocks	Buy Price	Buy Date	Return	Sold date
Apple (AAPL)	107.20	08/26/15	12%	10/19/15
Gilead Sciences (GILD)	105.94	08/26/15	-4%	
General Motors (GM)	27.69	08/26/15	12%	09/17/15
Genwealth Financial (GNW)	4.54	08/26/15	10%	08/27/15

Section IV: Market timing by Calendar

1   Market timing by calendar

The following predictions are based on historical data. You may have slightly different findings depending on when you start and when you end your testing.

You can load the historical data of SPY via Yahoo!Finance and check out how close you are or different from my own predictions. They are my predictions based on historical data. Use it as a reference only.

- Presidential cycle.
  Usually, the market performs worse in the first two years after the election than the next two. During the 3rd **year** the president has to make the economy look rosy in order to buy votes. Statistically it is the best year for the market and is followed by a good year (the election year). The government may stimulate the economy, the stock market and employment by printing more money, lowering interest rates and lowering taxes. The market in the 100 days before the election should be positive and less volatile according to 40 years of data. The next 100 days after the inauguration should be good for the market (termed as the honeymoon period).

  Democratic presidents have better market performance statistically than Republican presidents. This is not too logical as though Republicans are more pro-business traditionally.

- Olympics.
  It has been proven that the host country has a better chance that its stock market appreciates the year after the Olympics. It could be due to the exposure from the Olympics and / or the huge expenses in preparing for the Olympics. The last two Olympics follow this pattern as of 12/23/2013:

Olympics Country / Year	ETF	Period	Return
United Kingdom / 2012	EWU	Jan. 3, 2013 - Dec. 23,2013	11%
China / 2008	FXI	Jan. 3, 2009 - Dec. 31, 2009	43%

Greece could be an exception. It is too small a country to host this world-class event and it has wasted too many resources by building too many white elephants that the country can never justify. Brazil depends on its export of natural resources to China, so I do not count on the Olympics effect there. Japan 2020 was adversely affected by the pandemic.

Winning a lot of Olympic medals has no prediction for the stock markets. Both the Russian Empire and E. Germany were winners but disappeared in their original forms afterwards.

- Seasonal.
Best profitable investment period is: Nov. 1 to April 30 of the following year. It is similar to the saying 'Sell in May and Go away'. It has not worked since 2009 as it was an Early Recovery (defined by me) in the market cycle.

The market does not always happen as predicted. However, when more folks follow this, it becomes a self-fulfilling prophecy. I prefer "Sell on April 15 and come back on Oct. 15" to act before the herd. The more practical strategy is to start selling on April 1 and become more aggressive (selling at closer to the market prices) when it is close to May 1. For the last five years, I did not find this prediction reliable.

The explanation of the 'summer doldrums' could be that the investors cash their stocks for vacations and college tuition in the fall. Buying quality companies at the dips could be profitable.

- The worst month: September.
The next worst month is October. However, if there is no serious market crash during October (and this month has more than its shares of crashes), it could be the best month to buy stocks.

- The best month for the bull: November.
However, several market bottoms occurred in October and November. The next strong month is December. Most experts believe the best 3 months of the year starts in November.

- Best 30 days: Dec. 15 to Jan. 15, next year.

It was correct for the period of 2012-2013.

- Window dressing.
  Institutional investors sell their losers and buy winners around Nov. 1. From my rough estimate and on the average, the winners have a 2% percentage point gain better than the market and the losers have 1% worse than the market.

  I recommend that you evaluate the top 10 winners from the last 10 months or YTD on Oct. 15 and sell them at 3% gain or two months later.

  I recommend that you buy in Dec. and sell them 3 months later. Include the stocks with more than 30% loss for the last 11 months or YTD, sort them by Earning Yield in descending order and evaluate the top 10 stocks.

  In both cases, do not buy foreign stocks and stocks with return of capital. Ignore stocks not in the three major exchanges, with low volumes and stock prices less than $2. Do not buy in losing years such as 2007 and 2008. I have my tests with my own assumptions and I use tools not available to most readers. From my own experiences, I made more money by buying the losers from Dec. 15 to end of Dec. than buying the window dressers.

This is a guideline only. Do not buy any stocks during market plunges. Current events should be considered first such as a potential war and the hiking of interest rates.

Afterthoughts

- I predict it will be a sideways market in the later part of 2013. I am following the sideways strategy: Buy on dips and sell when the market is up. One's prediction.

- Why September has a bad reputation?
  http://www.marketwatch.com/story/betting-on-septembers-terrible-odds-2013-08-27?dist=beforebell

  September of 2013 (2 days away at the time of this writing) may have more problems. Check out how many of the following are correct on Oc. 1, 2013. Use it as a future guideline to predict the next September using the current market conditions then:

1. The market is not excessively expensive, but it is not cheap. It is due for a 5% correction.
2. Unrest in Syria (check any unrest in your next prediction in September).
3. High oil prices due to Syria.
4. September is statistically a bad month for the stock market. However, it could be an opportunity to invest after the correction if any.
5. Interest rates are rising.
6. All the above indicate the market will dip. However, the rosier outlook is that the global economies are improving even slowly.

- January effect.
  The performance of January may determine how the entire year performs. I cannot find any rationale but it has been proven right statistically.

- Earnings period announced in Jan., April, July and Oct. would cause big swings in stocks when they have surprises. Earning revisions could be a good predictor.
  http://www.investopedia.com/terms/e/earningsseason.asp

Links
Presidential Cycle:
http://www.investopedia.com/articles/financial-theory/08/presidential-election-cycle.asp
Calendar-based market timing:
http://stock-chartist.com/2010/10/calendar-based-market-timing/
Calendar market timing for 2013:
http://www.investorecho.com/archives/8047

2   Summary

I made the following charts so it is easier to time the market by the calendar.

All dates are inclusive.

No.	Metric		Score
1	Seasonal	Nov. - April, Score = 1	
2	Best Month	Nov., Score = 1	
		Sep., Score = -1	
3	Best Days	Dec. 15 – Jan.15 Score = 1	
4	Presidential Cycle	Election Year, Score = 1	
		1st Year in Office, Score = -1	
		2nd year, Score = -1	
		3rd year, Score = 2	
5	Presidential[3]	Democratic = 1 Republican = -1	
6	Market Cycle	Early Recovery, Score = 3	
		Up, Score = 2	
		Peak, Score = 1	
7	SPY (Finviz.com)	SMA200% > 8%[2] Score = -1	
		SMA200% < 0 Score = -1	
		RSI(14) > 65% Score = -1	
		Grand Score	

Footnote.
1   Refer to the Market Cycle chapter on how I define phases of a cycle.
2   For simplicity, use Finviz.com. Enter SPY and you will find SMA200% and RSI(14) to predict whether the market is peaking and overbought.
3   I'm politically neutral. The selection is based on historical statistics.

Add up all the scores. The passing grade is 0. According to my table which is based on my personal selections/preferences, the market is favorable when the grand score is 1 or higher. I bet it is the first time you see such a scoring system for market timing.

Sectors for market cycle

Market Phase[1]	Favorable		Unfavorable
Early Recovery	Financial, Technology, Industrial		Energy, Telecom, Utilities
Up	Technology, Industrial		
Peak	Mineral, Health Care, Energy		
Bottom	Consumer Staples, Utilities		Consumer Discretionary, Technology, Industrial
Seasonal	**Favorable**		**Unfavorable**
Winter	Energy, Utilities		
End of year	QQQ, EWG		
Olympics	ETF for host country[2]		

Footnote.
1   Refer to the Market Cycle chapter on how I define phases of a cycle.
2   Buy it next year after the Olympics. It could be due to higher GDP or the publicity. However, be selective. Greece is too small a country to host an Olympics.

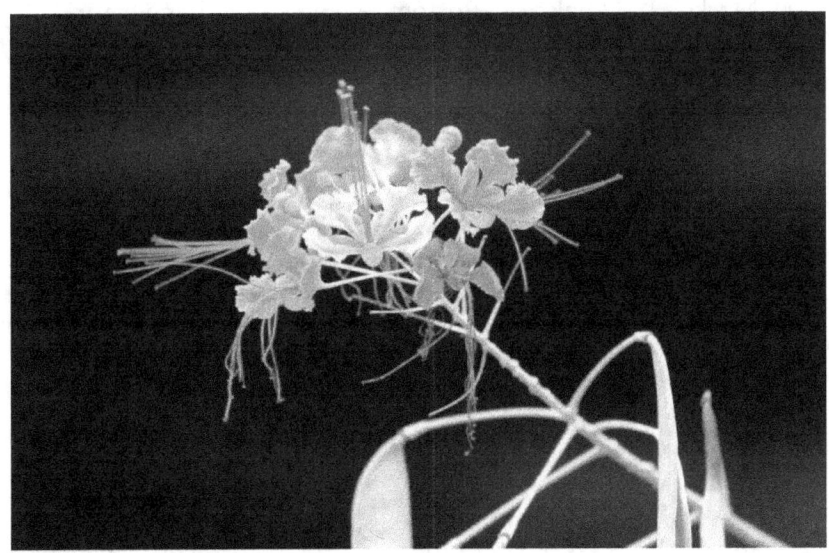

Section V: Peaks and bottoms

It will be great when we can sell at peaks and buy at bottoms. It is not that easy. However, I try to find the common characteristics of peaks and bottoms. No tools can detect them. Otherwise, there would be no poor folks. The following are my suggestions.

1   Market peaks / bottoms

Summary by tables from my findings

The dates could be a little different from my similar tables as I use monthly data instead of daily data. The data are subject to my interpretations and the tables are used for illustration purposes only.

Table: Market Plunges

Market Plunge	Months (Peak to Bottom)	Loss	Annualized Loss
2000	17	56%	40%
2007	25	47%	23%
Average	21	51%	31%

Table: Vital Dates

Market Plunge	Peak	Bottom	Indicator Exit	Indicator Reentry
2000	08/28/00	09/20/02	10/30/00	05/26/03
2007	10/12/07	03/06/09	01/03/08	09/08/09

Most investors were fully invested in 2007 and 2008 and NOT fully invested in 2009. It proves the majority of us are performing worse than the market. If you followed the exit indicator and the reentry indicator, you should do far better than the average investor. A brief exit and reentry in the 2007 market cycle is skipped for simplicity (I call it a false signal).

Market plunges

The SMA 350 (Single Moving Average for 350 trade sessions) has detected the last two crashes (2000 and 2007) correctly leaving us a lot of time to prepare. It is based on the falling market, so it will detect the next market plunge. However, we may not be that lucky to have plenty of time to prepare for it (selling most of our positions) as in the last two (2000 and 2007).

Market peaks and bottoms

From the above table, the chart does not spot the peak and the bottom as expected. We would make far more money when selling at the peak and buying at the bottom. A dream perhaps?

SMA and/or RSI would confirm that the market is close to its peak or bottom. I gathered their values for the last two peaks and bottoms and I summarized them in this article. It is based on limited data and we treat the conclusions as nothing more than useful guidelines.

SMA, SMA% and RSI

SMA-20 (Single Moving Average for the last 20 trade days), SMA-50, SMA-200 and RSI(14) are the indicators I used. Look them up on Investopedia.com if you are not familiar with how they are used. Most are available in Finviz.com by specifying SPY as the stock symbol.

SMA percentages measure how far away is the market from their respective moving average. If the SPY's SMA-200 is 100 and the stock price is 200, the SMA-200% is 100% over the moving average. It would indicate that the market may be peaking.

$$\text{SMA-200\%} = (\text{Stock Price} - \text{SMA}) / \text{SMA}$$
$$= (200 - 100) / 100 = 100\%$$

RSI(14) measures whether the market is over or under bought using the last 14 trade sessions.

For detecting market crashes, I still prefer SMA-350. SMA-20 is good for predicting the short-term trend of a stock, but not for the entire market.

Bring Finviz.com up from your browser and enter SPY (or any market ETF representing the majority of your stocks). The SMA-n percentages and RSI(14) are displayed.

Misc.

Advance / Decline (AD or Buy/Sell ration). When it is below 1, be careful that the market could be near the top even if the S&P 500 index is rising. The theory is that fund managers (who drive the market) believe the market is risky, they want to unload the small stocks. They still want to keep or even add the investment on blue chips, which they are easier to unload when the market crashes. It indicates the market could be near the top. It is similar to (# of stocks making new heights) – (# of stocks making new lows). If it is positive and the market is rising, the market could be still fine.

The market could be heading up from the bottom as indicated by the following technical indicators.

- RSI(14) from SPY or RSP is less than 30%.
- AD is less than .2
- With the previous sessions mostly in red candles, the market changes to a long green candle.
- Both SMA-20% and SMA-50% for the market index are positive, and SMA-20% is more positive than SMA-50%.

Findings

I include my findings in 3 sections: market timing for crashes, market timing for corrections and briefly on individual stocks, which have many other factors to consider.

I try to exit the market during market plunges (i.e., the stock price of SPY is below its SMA-350). My greed does not always allow me to do so entirely.

Market corrections provide opportunities to buy stocks. However, you need to accumulate cash in advance to take advantage of the temporary dips and prepare a list of stocks to buy at specified prices. For market plunges, we should not buy any stocks.

Market corrections of 5% happen about twice a year (or a 10% correction once a year), but its frequency varies. They are harder to detect, so do not leave the market totally. I prefer to keep less than

15% in cash to buy in the expected market dips. 2013 is a good year for stocks and in preparing for the corrections you could miss the opportunity of making more money.

Conclusion via a table

My test data are using SPY from 1-2000 to 2-2014. The following is from my own interpretation. Again, past information does not guarantee future performance. It just serves as a guideline.

	SMA-50	SMA-200	SMA-350	SMA50/ SMA200	RSI (14)
Market					
Peak		5%	9%	101%	65%
Bottom		-32%	-31%	78%	25%
Correction					
Peak	4%	6%	11%	102%	65%
Bottom	-5%	-6%	-7%	97%	26%
Stock					
Peak					70%
Bottom					30%

As explained, the market is plunging when the stock price of SPY is below its SMA-350 (i.e., the SMA-350% is negative). From my table, the market could be peaking when SMA-350 is 9% or above.

From the first glance, it is quite logical. At market peaks or temporary peaks, the SMA% is substantially over 0% and RSI(14) is far higher than the RSI(14) in the market bottoms.

Corrections are harder to determine. I have tested two times in different ways to determine corrections and the results are a little different.

The first method is to identify the peaks of the corrections and then get the averages of SMA-50%, SMA-200%, SMA-350% and the RSI(14).

The second approach is more complicated and more subjective to describe here. The above table is a combination of the two approaches.

The market is not always rational. Today's market is influenced by the low interest rates.

What to act

Everyone wants to sell at the peak and buy at the bottom. However, these technical indicators and my interpretation may not always work.

When the market is peaking

To illustrate, when SMA-350 is over 9% (i.e., SPY's stock price is 9% over its SMA for the last 350 trade sessions) and/or RSI(14) is over 65%, it may indicate the market is peaking and overbought. I recommend:

- Accumulate cash but less than 15% of your portfolio. The actual percent depends on your risk tolerance. For those who do not care much about market fluctuations or do not have the time to trade stocks, do not play market timing on corrections.

- Sell the stocks that have appreciated enough to meet your objectives and/or their appreciation potentials are less than the average of your portfolio. Preferably, sell the stock with less tax implications (such as those qualifying for long term capital gain in your taxable accounts).

  Alternatively, buy one stock for every two stocks you sell when the peak drags on.

- Do not buy any new stocks with the above exception.

- Enforce stop loss that turns your sell orders to market orders when they fall below specific prices. Adjust the stop orders when the stocks appreciate (but do nothing when they depreciate).

  My suggestion is using 5% stop loss and 10% stop loss for volatile stocks. To reduce excessive trading, you can use 10% and 15% instead. After the earnings announcement (available in Finviz), the stock would fluctuate far more than 5%, so adjust them before their earnings announcement dates.

When the market is bottoming

You want to reenter the market when the stock price for SPY (or other ETF simulating the market) is above the SMA-350. The following two suggestions when to reenter the market earlier. They are riskier but have better rewards if the guess is correct.

* Start to reenter the market when SMA-200% (the stock price is above the SMA-200) is positive.
* Start to reenter the market when SMA-350% is less than -31% and/or RSI(14) is less than 25%, it may indicate the market is bottoming and under-bought.

Do the following:
* Buy the stocks that have the best appreciation potential and most are fundamentally sound and beaten up badly by the general market. Alternatively, buy two stocks for every stock you sell.
* Do not sell any stocks with the above exception.
* You need to prepare a list of stocks to buy and at what prices when the market is plunging. If you do not have such a list, buy ETFs.

What to do in a market correction
It is very similar to market timing on crashes as above. However, I recommend keeping cash to less than 15% of your portfolio. Again, corrections are far harder to detect. 2013 has fewer and smaller corrections due to the excessive supply of money.

Stocks

Stocks are treated as overbought when the RSI(14) is over 70% and under-bought when it is below 30%; most stocks fluctuate more than the market. Some may use 65% for overbought and 35% for under-bought.

Depending on how long you usually keep a stock, you select the number of days in SMA. For example, if you keep most stocks for 200 days, use SMA-200. Buy when the range of its SMA-200% is ranging from 0 to 10% and the RSI is less than 60% as a rough guideline.

Some stocks may just shoot up disregarding their fundamental and technical metrics. One's opinion. Selecting the SMA percent also depends on your risk tolerance. There are many other factors to consider on individual stocks such as a major lawsuit(s), losing/gaining market share... Again, use the above as a very rough guideline for the stocks.

Afterthoughts

- You will find many related articles on this topic by searching using Google.
- As of 3/5/2014, the market was supposed to be peaking as SMA-350% was 15% and RSI(14) was 73%. The historical data for these metrics can be shown on charts.
- Articles on market top.
  Business Insider.
  The flow to equity is a good contrary indicator (the more money goes to equity funds by retail investors, the more chance the market will plunge).
  http://www.businessinsider.com/signs-this-is-not-a-market-peak-2013-12
  The 15 signs.
  http://theeconomiccollapseblog.com/archives/15-signs-that-we-are-near-the-peak-of-an-absolutely-massive-stock-market-bubble

2   Peaking and Overbought

This chapter is an extension of the last one. The following indicators are not very reliable and they should be used as secondary indicators. However, exiting from the peak could make you more money if the signal is correct. When the price is 9% over the simple moving average SMA-350, the market may be peaking. This ratio is defined by:
(Price – Moving Average) / Moving Average.

When the RSI(14) is over 65%, the market could be overbought (i.e., highly valued). This ratio can be found in Finviz.com with SPY or another ETF that represents the market as the stock symbol. It is defined as:
RSI = 100 - 100/(1 + RS)

where RS = Average of x days' up closes / Average of x sessions
RSI(14) is the relative strength index using the last 14 trade sessions.

The reentry point is less than -31% for the SMA-350 ratio and less than 25% for the RSI(14). Again, they are used for a guideline only.

Suggested Actions
Peaking and overbought conditions indicate the market is overvalued. My suggestion is not to sell all positions except those stocks that are overvalued or have met your objectives. Place stop orders to protect profits. I recommend 5% below the current price and 10% for volatile stocks (10% and 15% are fine in today's volatile market). When the stock price rises, change the stop orders accordingly. When the stock is sold, accumulate cash until these conditions change.

I recommend using the cash to buy CDs and short-term, bonds that are investment grade. Save some cash to buy contra ETFs when the market is plunging. 2008 was not a good year for bonds, but 2009 was. Based on this, I would sell the bonds when the market is crashing. Investing is not a 100% sure thing. These are my recommendations and you need to modify the plan according to your risk tolerance.

3   Design a test for market peaks/bottoms

This article describes how to set up a test for the last article on detecting market peaks/bottoms by using SMA and RSI. There is no need to understand how I derived the results and it could serve as a model for designing a test for another strategy.

Objective
To find out any common values of SMA and RSI when the market plunges, corrects or surges.

The data for this test are obtained from Yahoo!Finance and/or charts available from many other free sites.

How to get data

From Yahoo!Finance, enter SPY for the stock. Select historical prices from 1/3/96 to 2/5/14 in my example. Use the prices adjusted for splits and dividends; in this case it may not make any difference. Load it to Excel. Sort the date in the ascending order. Delete the columns I do not need.

Adjusted Close Price is mostly the one you want to use for testing to compensate for the split and dividend.
https://help.yahoo.com/kb/finance/SLN2311.html?impressions=true

Most historical databases do not include dividends but handle splits. Hence, we have to adjust accordingly. Add the dividend rate (about 1.75%) to the annualized return rate where appropriate.

Get critical dates
I limited my test data to the last two crashes (2000 and 2007). The test data before 2000 may not reflect today's market. Here are the critical dates from my other book.

Table: Vital Dates

Market Plunge	Peak	Bottom	Indicator Exit	Indicator Reenter
2000	08/28/00	09/20/02	10/30/00	05/26/03
2007	10/12/07	03/06/09	01/03/08	09/08/09

Get statistics on previous peaks and bottoms

To illustrate, the peak in 2000 is 08/28/00, calculate the SMA-200, SMA-350, SMA-50 and SM50/SMA200 for this date. Actually, I included 4 days before and 4 days after and averaged all the mentioned parameters for a total of 9 days. Try to automate this procedure as much as possible.

Repeat the above for 2007. Average the parameters in the two market plunges.

Repeat the same for the two market bottoms.

RSI(14)

There is too much logic to calculate this indicator. I used the RSI from charts for the critical dates. Select RSI in the chart.

Filler: OTC, cars and filthy rich in 5 seconds

OTC, over-the-counter stocks, are risky as many do not have information required by SEC and the major exchanges. They are traded over the counter, OTC. They cannot be shorted (and most likely you do not want to do so even if it was allowed). Pier 1, Ford, American Airlines and many others were all penny stocks.

Expect one winner for several losers. However, the total profit could outpace the total loss if the strategy is properly implemented.

Filler: Advances in cars
I have not used cruise control even ONCE. I could be the exception. The more complex the car, the more chance it breaks down.

A few years ago, I got an on-line statement from my broker saying I had over 10M. I took a screenshot. When I logged off and logged on again, my millions were gone and so were many better things in life I planned to buy. What a tough life! I try to say the car computer could break down too and it may cause lives.

4 Market peak example

It is hard to determine market peaks and bottoms. Otherwise, there would be no poor folks. Based on data from 7/4/2017, I tried to predict (again predict) whether the market is peaking.

From my previous findings:

Table: Market Plunges

Market Plunge	Months (Peak to Bottom)	Loss	Annualized Loss
2000	17	56%	40%
2007	25	47%	23%
Average	21	51%	31%

Table: Vital Dates

Market Plunge	Peak	Bottom	Indicator Exit	Indicator Reentry
2000	08/28/00	09/20/02	10/30/00	05/26/03
2007	10/12/07	03/06/09	01/03/08	09/08/09

My test data uses the SPY from 1-2000 to 2-2014 to get the averages of the peaks. The following is from my own interpretation. Again, past information does not guarantee future performance. It just serves as a guideline.

	SMA-50	SMA-200	SMA-350	SMA50/ SMA200	RSI (14)
Market (SPY)					
Peak (avg.)		5%	9%	101%	65%
7/4/2017	0%	6%	10%	N/A	50%

Both SMA-200% and SMA-350% are on par with the averages of the previous two market peaks. RSI(14) shows the market is overbought but it is 15% less than the average. I missed some parameters such as P/E. The P/E as of 7/4/17 is 25.69 and is about 71% more expensive assuming the average is 15. The average of 11 stocks from Fidelity's best sector list increased by only 0.35% for last month. So, it is not a good sign.

Fundamental metrics (07/20/2017)

	L.T. Avg.	7/20/ 17	High by[1]	Min	On	Max	On
P/E[2]	15.66	26.17	67%	5.31	12-1917	123.73	05-2017
Shiller P/E[2]	16.76	30.12	80%	4.78	12-1920	44.19	12-1999
P/Sales[2]	1.45	2.15	48%	0.8	03-2009	2.15	07-2017
P/Book[2]	2.75	3.22	17%	4.78	12-1920	44.19	12-1999

[1] High by = (Current – Mean) /Mean

[2] From http://www.multpl.com/.

The market is fundamentally overvalued as indicated in 07/04/2017.

The transport index (DJT) could be an indicator too. It loses its luster due to web sales not depending on rails and trucks.

Read articles on the current market such as this one.
https://www.marketwatch.com/story/the-biggest-problem-in-the-stock-market-bullishness-is-clouding-investors-thinking-2020-08-27?mod=home-page

Section VI: Miscellaneous

1   A sideways market

The market moves up or down. Usually, it dances sideways when switching from one trend to the other. When it moves down, it moves at a faster speed. When the volume is unusually low, it could be a hint that the market is changing direction on me.

Market movements could be predicted by moving averages (30-days moving average is one for dips and 52 weeks for plunges for example). When it moves above the average line, most likely it will move up and vice versa.

For volatile markets, the last time it peaks and the last time it bottoms are termed as **resistance lines and support lines** respectively. In theory and theory only, a sideways market never breaks out from these two lines. It is a prediction only and many other factors should be considered. Even with all the right educated guesses, the market is not always rational.

Take advantage of the sideways movements by buying at small dips (the support line) and selling at small peaks (the resistance line).

You can take advantage of market timing by not holding a stock forever and by buying and selling the same stock or an ETF. I believe the 'buy-and-hold' idea has been dead since 2000. I cannot find too many articles praising this strategy with data after 2000.

Market plunges are usually fast and steep.

2015 Update. The last time we had a down year in a year before the election year was 1939, the start of WW2. Even 2007 was an up year. I had posted this info for 2015 even during the fierce correction in August, 2015. Adding the 1.9% dividend, the market beats the one-year CD by a good margin in 2015. To profit in this market, buy at temporary dips and sell at temporary surges.

Links

Resistance line and support line:
http://en.wikipedia.org/wiki/Support_and_resistance

2   Market timing by asset class

Two major trading strategies are:
1. Buy high and sell higher.

   It is a kind of momentum play. You may keep these stocks for less time (say, less than three months). The momentum could change very fast. In my momentum portfolio, I keep most of my stocks for less than a month.
2. Buy low and sell high.

   When the asset class is totally out-of-favor and it has high value, buy it. It is a value play. You are swimming against the tide. You need to hold these stocks longer (say, longer than 6 months) for the market to realize its value.

It is not possible to predict correctly the peaks and bottoms of any asset class consistently. However, #1 usually starts first and is followed by #2. The holding period is just a suggestion.

Your success will be improved by using technical analysis correctly. Try the 50-day moving average (actually the last 50 trade sessions) to start with. Buy when it is above the moving average and sell when it is below. Next, try the 20-day moving average and many other technical analysis indicators such as exponential moving average and different days for the moving averages. The moving averages are available from Finviz.com without charting.

Basically, there is a tradeoff on switching too frequently and reacting too late. Some stocks are more volatile than others.

Try out different asset classes such as gold and oil. To illustrate, no one can predict that a gold price at $1800 is the peak. If you buy gold coins at $1000 and ride the gold wagon to $1600, you're doing quite well. In this case, trade GLD, the ETF fund for gold for technical analysis. The way to protect your profit and let the profit rise is using stops. Adjust the stop when the asset appreciates.

My experience in gold

I had gold coins bought at about $400 each many years ago. Gold did not appreciate much for over 20 years. When its price rose to $800, I sold some. I made a 100% return, but it may not even beat inflation. If I invested in stocks instead of gold coins, I would be far better off in total return (appreciation plus dividends). When gold rose to $1000, I sold more. Our rational thinking (part of human nature) would not allow us to hold these coins until $1,800. The moral is no one can predict the peak value of an asset and act accordingly.

Trading coins in your local shops would cost you a lot (commission and the spread) but it is safer. The coin shops do report your sales to the IRS if the sell is below a certain amount. Check the current rules.

Links
Disadvantages of gold ETFs:
https://www.youtube.com/watch?v=wMxj6iB92ZA

3   My predictions

Recently I read several books on how several authors claimed their correct predictions on the housing bubble in 2007. I do not know whether it is before the fact or after the fact. At least two authors made similar predictions on the bubbles of the stock market after 2008.

So far they have either not materialized or have been just wrong. If you followed them to move all the stocks into cash, you have missed the biggest recovery of the stock market from 2009 to today (12-2015). The excessive printing of money boosts the stock market even though the economy has not been totally recovered.

It taught us:

- The correct prediction of one major event does not mean his/her future predictions will be correct even with good arguments.
- Even authors of best-seller books could be just a one-trick pony. I was amused that at least two authors blamed other authors of being a one-trick pony while they were one themselves.

I had the best performance in 2009 and recovered most if not all of my loss in 2007. I was too conservative after 2009. As of 7/2013, I would like to review which of my predictions are right.

This chapter is for information and education purposes. I have not spent enough time to evaluate every one of my predictions. The primary purpose is:

- With educated guesses, we should have more right than wrong. A win percentage of over 50% can make you a lot of money.
- Buying stocks or any investment is a prediction for better profit potential. Hence, there are risks that the prediction will not materialize.
- Learn from good experiences and bad experiences. However, ensure the lesson is not due to an irrational market, luck and conditions you cannot control.

- Even with the best arguments, the prediction may never materialize. Do not bet the entire farm on it.
- Your actions depend on your risk tolerance.

Correct or close to correct predictions

- 2000 market plunge. Moved most of my high-tech sectors to traditional industries. It could be better to move them to cash or contra ETFs (I believe they were not available in 2000).
- 2003. Moved back to stocks for better profit in Early Recovery.
- 2009. Moved back to stocks in Early Recovery. I had my best return in my largest taxable account by dipping into my credit line (not recommended).
- 2011. My prediction was very close and better than most other predictions for that year. Same for 2012.
- April, 2012 Correction. Quite close.
- June, 2013 Correction. It was a 6% correction, not the predicted 10%.
- Some stock winners (more winners due to the rising market and scoring system). Scoring System works by beating the market for the test period.
- Recommended Apple at 390.50 (before the split) on 5-2013.

Incorrect predictions

- 2008 market plunge.
  It was due to my false security on huge profits from energy stocks. When the economy continued heading south in 2008, everything including my energy stocks plunged. The simple chart from the chapter on Spotting Big Plunges should help. I did not use it as I had not discovered and refined this simple technique.

- Correction on Q1 2013.
  There was no correction. It could be due to the pumping of too much money in the market by the government. As of 8/2013, my stocks performed quite well. However, I've been keeping too much cash expecting a serious correction. It is a case of winning the battles but losing a war.

- Some stocks were losers. I did not learn from my previous findings to avoid these stocks.

The prediction for all predictions

The chart in Detecting Market Plunges shows you how to follow the moving average to exit the market and reenter the market. It works splendidly in the last two market plunges (2000 to 2015). It will work for the future plunges. However, the charts may not provide plenty of time to react as the last two; only time can tell.

Summary

It is not important about how many times we have predicted right, but what we have learned from our good and bad predictions. Learn from our experience and that would help us to make better future predictions. All our stock trading decisions are based on predictions. Some will materialize and some will not. Diversify your portfolio.

#Filler:

The golden rules on market plunges heard from the street:

Rule #1: Anything can go wrong; the market is irrational.

Rule #2: The market falls 3 times faster than it rises most of the time.

Rule #3: You have to gain 100% to rectify a 50% loss.

Rule #4: The easier the rules of the market game, the fewer will want to play.

Rule #5. Retail investors buy at the top due to greed.

Rule #6. Retail investors sell at the bottom due to the fear that the market will never return but it always does.

Fidelity
Click on "News & Research" and then "Stock Market & Sector Performance" for Equity Market Commentary.

4   Reasons for the Coming Market Crash

This is an **example** for 2021 only. For the last few years, most market predictors have had their crystal balls broken. It is due to the excessive supply of money that leads to a non-correlation of the economy and the stock market. It cannot last forever. It will correlate again when the money supply is reduced.

The incredible recovery of the market from 2007-8 is due to the excessive printing of money (i.e., money supply). History is repeated again in 2020. It leads to easy credit to buy stock (margin debt) and buyouts/corporate profits. With more money to buy stocks and fewer stocks to buy (buyouts), it is a simple case of Supply and Demand.

Since World War II, we never had a down year in a year just before the election including 2007 and 2019. However, 2021 could be a tough year and the market bubble may finally burst. As usual, there are two camps arguing in opposite directions for predicting the market direction of 2021. I recommend my readers to take some actions, the same as buying insurance. As of 1/2021, the market is unsound fundamentally but sound technically. When the technical is unsound, it is the time to leave the market as indicated by the simple market timing illustrated in this book.

Consult your financial advisor before taking any actions, and I am not responsible for your gains or losses.

Good News

- We have hopes on the ending of this pandemic at least reducing the impact in 2021.

- The economy is improving slowly except in some sectors that are affected immensely by the pandemic.

- Energy cost could be bottom that is good for the energy sector. Judging by the forward P/Es of many energy companies, I do not believe green energy would take over in 2021.

- The interest rate is almost zero that is good for the housing sector and related sectors, buybacks, margin interest rate and investing by the corporations.

Bad News

- It has been one of the longest bull markets.
- The economy is poor compared to one year ago with high unemployment rate.
- Many small businesses such as restaurants will be closed for ever.
- The record-high market is a bubble to many.
- Margin debt is in the record high.
- The government is running out of tools to revive the economy such as lowering interest rate. Excessive supplying of money will hurt the economy in the longer term.
- The national debts (partly due to our endless wars) and obligations (partly due to our aging population) are high as a percentage of the GDP.
- Most foreign countries except Japan have been reducing buying our national debt. Most of the debts were purchased by the Fed by printing money excessively.
- Many retailers that cannot service their debts will bankrupt if not already.
- The USD is weak and the status of a reserve currency is shaken. However, a weak USD is good for export, but not good for the profit for global companies.
- I expect higher inflation is coming.

Summary

2021 could be very risky. We're living dangerously on borrowed time. Hence, be conservative. The recent rise of the market is due to supply (excessive printing of money) and the demand (fixed number of assets). The market is not rational compared to the economy.

5   A simple but risky strategy on market timing

Follow the article "Simplest Market Timing" to time the market. If it tells you the market is going down, buy contra ETFs and/or move stocks to cash depending on your risk tolerance.

Recommended ETFs (5 total)
SPY
PSQ
SEF
GLD
Money Market / CD

My reasons

Contra ETFs are betting the sectors represented to go down. During a market downturn, I would bet against bank/financial stocks (SEF, a contra ETF for the financial sector) and tech stocks (PSQ, a contra ETF for NASDAQ which includes a lot of tech stocks).

GLD is an ETF for gold. During a recession, gold should fare better than stocks, but it may not perform most of the contra ETFs. If the value of the USD depreciates, gold would fare better. Every portfolio should have 2 to 10% in gold depending on your risk tolerance. If you are conservative, move everything to Money Market fund / CD instead of the contra ETFs when the market is crashing.

We have only one false alarm from 2000 to 2010 but more after 2010. The false alarm tells you to exit the market and then tells you to reenter the market shortly. If you do not buy any contra ETFs, most likely you do not lose much.

After the crash
When the market timing tells you to return to the market, sell contra ETFs and buy SPY (or any ETF that simulates the market) and value stocks. You need more time to find and evaluate value stocks, so buy SPY first. Use stops to protect your portfolio.

Book 3 (bonus): Technical Analysis (TA)

Technical analysis (TA) is the analysis of the price movements and the short-term trend and possible reversal, while fundamental analysis focuses on metrics such as price/earnings ratio and debts. TA assumes the future stock price behavior can be determined by the patterns of past price behavior – it is true more times than untrue. Traders use TA a lot and can profit by shorting stocks. Investors can use them to find the entry points and exit points and some investors only buy stocks with a positive long-term trend (using SMA-200%).

Many times stock analysis based on fundamentals fails when the evaluation is solely based on fundamentals. Technical Analysis (TA) has the following characteristics:

- Most of the time, TA is profitable in the short term (less than 3 months). The weather man is more accurate in tomorrow's weather rather than a month away. TA can also signal the reversals.
- There are too many signals if you have more than three TA parameters. To start, use SMA (Simple Moving Average) and RSI(14); both are available in Finviz.com without charting.
- You can combine TA with fundamentals such as a rising SMA50 with increasing Insider Purchases. In addition, you can use more than one TA indicator.
- For market timing, TA is a huge part, but many fundamentals should be considered too. You can use similar techniques to time the market and time stocks and/or sectors such as Golden Cross / Death Cross.

Technical analysis wins for the following reasons:
- Information such as a new product or a major lawsuit pending is not reflected timely in fundamentals, but rather in technical analysis. It gives us guidance in understanding the trend of a stock or even the entire market.
- Most TAs are based on accumulated data. For example, if RSI(14) is greater than 65, most likely this stock is overbought. If there is no reason for this condition, you may consider selling it.
- When too many investors follow TA, it would become self-prophecy.

- Do not act against the trend. The fundamentalist may buy a stock when it loses 50%, the TA investor most likely will not buy it. Many times the losing stocks will lose another 25% or so. The TA investor most likely buys it on the way up only or short it on the way down.

An example. NVRO (a stock symbol) has appreciated about 100% from mid Feb. to Oct. in 2016 despite its poor fundamentals. It has a new product that could revolutionize physical healing and eliminate pain that will not be shown in the fundamentals except by the eventual Forward P/E. Technical charts can inform us of the uptrend.

Volume is the confirmation. Institution investors drive the market. When the market (esp. the S&P 500 stocks) is down and the volume is up, there is good chance institution investors are dumping their holdings. It is obvious when most of the indicators are promising but the volume is small.

Info from free websites.
Use "Head and shoulder" as an example. Obtain the description by typing "Head and shoulder" in Investopedia. Obtain more info by entering same in the search under YouTube.

Links:
Before you trade:
https://www.youtube.com/watch?v=8hM18AHcUCs
A strategy: https://www.youtube.com/watch?v=asDBegQaupM

1   Technical analysis (TA)

The basics
Technical analysis (a.k.a. charting) is easier to learn than you might expect. It represents the trend of the market (a stock or a group of stocks) graphically. If more investors are in the market, the market would move upwards until it changes direction. We divide the trends into short-term, intermediate-term and long-term.

The chartists usually do not consider fundamentals as they believe they have already been priced into the stock price and some fundamentals are not available to the public. To illustrate, a new drug has been discovered, the stock price of the company jumps initially by insiders purchases and the informed. Its fundamental metrics do not demonstrate this right away, but many investors are buying to boost up the stock price as evidenced by the technical indicators such as SMA for 20 or 50 days.

The volume is a confirmation. When the stock moves up or down by 10% with a low volume, the trend is not yet confirmed.

The trend of the stock price is not a straight line in most cases. Hence a trend line is usually drawn to indicate the direction of the stock. Many investors believe the stocks fluctuate in certain ranges (i.e., channels) and the chart draws the upper value (the resistance line) and the lower value (the support line). In theory, the price of a stock fluctuates within the resistance line (ceiling for understanding) and support (floor). When it reaches its support, it becomes a buy and vice versa for a sell. Most charts including Finviz.com would display these lines.

When the price passes out of the channel, it is called a breakout. Darvas, one of the oldest and most successful chartists, profited from the breakouts of the resistance line and believed the stock was close to the support line of the new channel. Hence it would be a long way up in theory.

If it were so simple, there will be no poor folks
It works most of the time, but do not place all your money on it. For chartists, 51% is great (the same for playing Black Jack). Some trends reverse very fast such as the bio drug stocks in 2015. You need to hedge your bets such as placing stop orders. Most do not want to spend their lives watching the trend from a big screen.

Most novices use too many technical indicators and lose in their performances to the professionals. Recently, most chartists were not doing all that great and I did not find many books on their success than a decade ago. It could be due to too many followers in similar setups. I verified it with my recent testing using Finviz.com.

Simple Moving Average
The basic technical indicator is SMA-N. It is the average of the last N trade sessions. To illustrate, if N is 15 and the exchange is open

during this period, you need 3 weeks (21 days) of data. When N is 20 (or SMA-20), we classify it as short-term. Similarly, SMA-50 is an intermediate-term and SMA-200 is long-term. I prefer 50, 100 and 250. This trend duration is important. For example, do not want to place long-term purchases using the short-term SMA-50. There are many modifications to SMA such as giving more weight to recent data, but I have not found them any better. Finviz.com includes this information without charting (SMA-20, SMA-50 and SMA-100 in percentages).

Defining the trend periods is rather arbitrary. I use SMA-350 to detect the market plunges and SMA-100 for stocks. Weighted Moving Average weighs more weight on recent price data.

It can be used to determine whether we are in a bull, a bear or a sideways market using SMA-50 (or SMA-200 for longer term) for the market (using SPY), the sector (using an ETF for the sector and the specific stock. The trend is up when the price is above the SMA and the reversal of the trend.
https://www.youtube.com/watch?v=jdYNaE5GJOk

The trend is your best friend
Most traders use TA for trending in a short duration. Investors can also use TA to time the entry and exit points for better potential profits. Value investors usually are patient and they do bottom fishing and they search for 'oversold' conditions using RSI(14). Again, high volume is a confirmation.

Many sites provide charting free of charge such as Yahoo!Finance. Finviz.com provides a lot of technical indicators without charting such as SMA% and RSI(14). It also provides screen searching for stocks that meet your technical analysis criteria.

Hands on
Bring up Finviz.com and enter any stock symbol such as AAPL. You can see the daily prices of AAPL from about nine months ago to today. Three SMAs (Simple Moving Average) are displayed as SMA-20, SMA-50 and SMA-200. The first two are for short-term trends. When the price is above the SMA, it is expected to be trending up. Again, the trade volume is used as a confirmation

You can also see the resistance line and the support line drawn. In theory, the stock will trade within these lines. When it exceeds its resistance line, it is called a breakout, and vice versa for a breakdown. Sometimes it displays some technical patterns such as Cup and Shoulder and Double Down (both are positive patterns).

Select Weekly data. The Candle chart is better described than the Daily chart. Candles give us better descriptions of the price: open, close, high and low. The green color indicates the price is up for the period (a week in this example) and the red color indicates a down period.

In addition, Finviz.com includes some technical indicators in the metric section such as RSI. Most other chart sites are similar in the basics. Use Finviz's Help and select Technical Analysis for more description. Investopedia has enhanced descriptions on this topic.

TA patterns
There are many TA patterns such as Bollinger Bands and MACD. The patterns are based on the stock prices and many times they prove to be correct predictions especially on stocks with high volume and high market caps. Patterns have been repeating themselves many times as they are driven by investors.

Sites for TA
There are many free sites for charts with explanations of their technical indicators. Popular ones include BigCharts.com, SmallCharts.com and Yahoo!Finance. Fidelity includes some unique features in its charts such as P/E.

Why I do not use TA as a primary tool for stock picking
My investing style is different from a day trader. I prefer to 'Buy Low and Sell High' instead of 'Buy High and Sell Higher'. I try to find the real bottom price. TA will not find the bottom very easily but it tracks the trend better. As a bargain hunter, I do not expect the stock will rise fast as I'm usually swimming against the tide. However, value stocks could stay in the low price for a long time (i.e., value trap). I like to select stocks that turn around as evidenced by the SMA-20 and SMA-50.

With that said, my momentum portfolio has appreciated consistently and usually has the best performing stocks among all my portfolios. It is based on the timely grade from my subscriptions plus the metrics on TA timing.

Most chartists would also tell you to buy the stocks that have broken out (i.e., higher than the resistance line) and/or stocks at their highs. Contrary to value investing, you should exit when the trend reverses. The reversal could happen very fast and hence protect your portfolio by setting up stop loss (preferably with trailing stop) orders.

My opinion. I do not want to argue whether TA is good for you or not. You need to find that out. Most likely, the day traders and very short-term traders will profit more from TA than the investors seeking value stocks for the long-term gains.

Random remarks
Even if you do not use technical analysis, you should spend some time learning it. It is better to marry fundamentals and TA. My random remarks are:

- The Institutional investors (insurance companies, pension funds, mutual funds, etc.) use TA and they MOVE the market. A lot of times it becomes a self-fulfilling prophecy. It is better to join them as most of us cannot beat them.
- Day traders take advantage of the institutional investors by spotting their trends and jumping on the wagon.
- Most TA stocks should be good sized and have large average daily volumes. I prefer to use TA on value stocks to prevent long-term losses.
- I do know some folks making big money using TA, but I know more making good money using fundamentals. Since TA predicts the market better in the shorter term, its practitioners may have to pay higher taxes (in today's tax laws) in taxable accounts.
- Our objective should be making money with the least risk. Once you claim to belong to a certain group of either Fundamental or TA, you will be biased and forget your primary objective in investing.
- TA tracks the last two big market plunges (2000 and 2007) pretty well. The chart will not warn you right away for the upcoming plunge (as it depends on past data) to avoid the initial losses, but they will warn you to avoid bigger losses.

- You can use TA to short the stock, the sector, the country or the market.
- Risk management (with stops to reduce losses and trailing stops for rising stocks) and trade positions (more positions on stocks with better potential) could make you a fortune, even if you have only 50% correct.
- Your desire, passion, discipline, knowledge and hand-on skill (including learning from your successes and failures) are the keys to success. A well-tested strategy and TA tools to time the trend of a stock, sector and the market are the tools.

Afterthoughts
Besides searching for stocks that have potential breakouts, we should check the stocks we own for potential breakdowns.
Technical Analysis tutorial.
https://www.YouTube.com/watch?v=GENBVwV8PMs

SMA tutorial.
https://www.YouTube.com/watch?v=Na-ctpPsnks

Links
Fidelity video: Technical Analysis
https://www.fidelity.com/learning-center/technical-analysis/chart-types-video

2   Examples of using TA

I have outlined how we can spot market plunges using TA and I use it to monitor the market every three months or so (I recommend doing it every month and even more frequently when the market is risky). Here is an example of how to use it to trade individual stocks.

I have to admit I do not use TA that much on individual stocks and clearly I am not an expert in TA. If this article stirs up your interest, read more books or attend seminars / classes on TA. However, this book describes the basic and most useful technical indicators. There are many good and free articles from Investopedia on this topic. Personally, I prefer to seek fundamentally sound companies at bargain prices and wait for their full appreciation. It has been proven to me many times over.

TA is very useful for momentum and day traders. With the rising volume, you can detect that the stocks are traded by managers of mutual funds, hedge funds, insurance companies and pension funds, and you profit by riding on their wagons.

Some stocks are good for TA. Usually, they are larger companies with above-average volumes and are fundamentally sound. Avoid the stocks that are trending downwards unless you're bottom fishing. Let me pick CSCO (a cyclical stock) for an illustration. I bought it several times in 2012. I sold some in 2013 and 2014 making good profits. This is quite different from what short-term traders would use during the following:

The green line is a 50-day simple moving average (SMA) for the following chart using one year data.

Buy the stock when it is above its SMA and sell when it is below. Following the chart would make good money based on this simple rule. Also, practice the strategy "Sell on May 1, Buy back on Nov. 1".

Not all stocks follow this profitable pattern. Fundamentalists may try to pick the bottom in late July while chartists enter positions on its upward trend. The chartists have an advantage to stay away from stocks in their downward trend.

Exponential Moving Average has better predictable power as it weighs more on recent prices. Some indicators / patterns work better in specific market conditions – all markets are different.

Volume is important as a confirmation. If the price of a stock is up with thin volume, the rise is questionable and it could be manipulated.

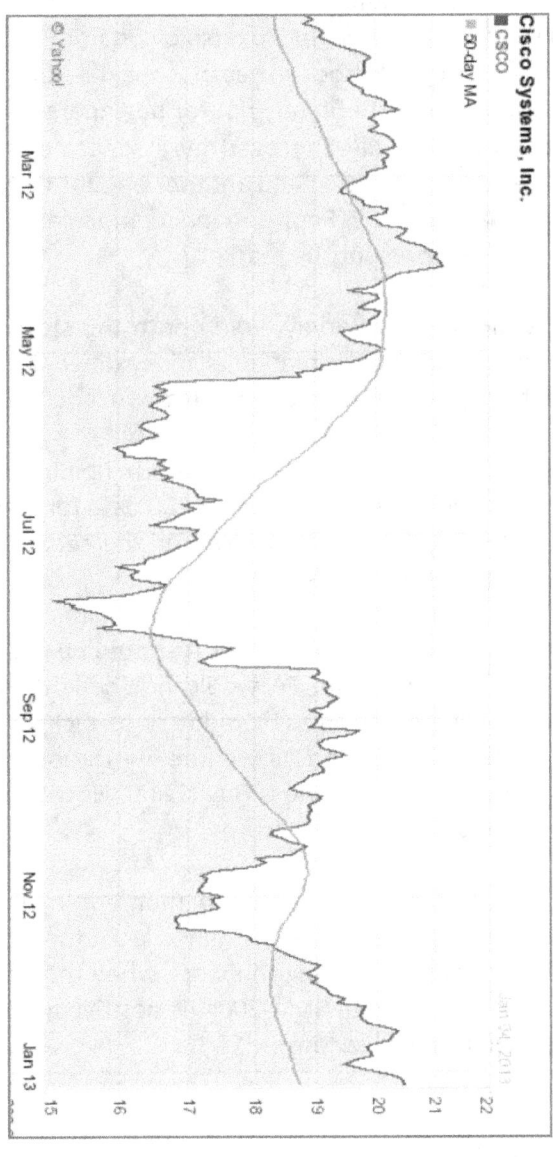

Table: CSCO 50-day SMA   Source: Yahoo!Finance
(https://ebmyth.blogspot.com/2020/09/table-csco-50-day-sma.html)

We can improve the trades by:

- Use a different moving average in the number of days (50 in this example) and other indicators such as EMA (a moving average that weighs higher on more recent data). It may improve prediction accuracy and/or cut down on the number of trades. RSI(14) suggests overbought / oversold conditions.
- Instead of selling the stock for cash, consider selling the stock short. Selling short is definitely not for beginners.
- The accuracy is usually improved by a separate chart for the sector the stock belongs to and another one for the market. For CSCO, you can use an ETF for network companies and SPY (or a similar ETF) to represent the market.

In theory and in theory only, when both the stock, the sector that the stock is in and the market all move down, the stock price has a high chance that it would move down, and vice versa.

We use the 50 days (in SMA) for short-term holding of stocks (20 for even shorter holding periods and 200 days for longer holding periods). Personally, I use 30 days for the sector ETF. Again, 'Days' is actually 'Trade Sessions'.

TA is not for most fundamentalists but it should be used
For a bargain hunter like me, TA would not benefit me a lot for picking stocks at their bottoms. I would try to pick up CSCO with prices ranging from 15-17 and all well below the moving average line, but TA would not show me a Buy signal. However, for short-term swing traders TA is a Godsend.

To me, TA is a good indicator for growth, momentum and for short-term trading. Some fundamentalists may use TA for entry and exit points. Some recommend buying the stock when the price is above the SMA-200 (same as when SMA-200% is positive and that can be readily obtained from Finviz.com).

It should be profitable for using the 'Buy High and Sell Higher' strategy, provided you protect your profits effectively. This is also called 'Buy at a reasonable cost'. One's opinion.

In selecting a tool, you have to understand how, and why to use it and whether it fits your investing style. I use TA for market timing for the entire market more than on individual stocks. When I have more time, I probably would use TA more frequently.

Most of us cannot spot the bottom of a stock; I have had some success but most likely they were due to luck. When a stock is moving up from the bottom, there is a good chance it will move further up. TA shows it and the volume confirms it.

Conclusion

Even a fundamentalist like me can benefit a lot by using TA. This book touches on the very basics of TA.

Besides monitoring the fundamentals of the stocks you bought once every 6 months, you should analyze their technical indicators more often (1 month to 3 months depending on your available time). When the market is risky (close to the SMA average), run the SMA chart more frequently (say once a week).

Rule-based   trading:
https://www.youtube.com/watch?v=GAH9EyydEsM

3   Easy TA without charts

Bring up Finviz.com from your browser. Enter the stock you're evaluating. SMA-200% stands for Simple Moving Average of the last 200 trade sessions. RSI(14)% is the relative strength index for the last 14 trade sessions.

The following is just a suggestion with conservative parameters. Adjust the parameters according to your risk tolerance and requirements. Do not buy the stock with SMA-200% is < 0 (trending down), SMA-200% > 40 (peaking), or RSI(14)% > 65 (overbought).

Link: RSI: https://www.youtube.com/watch?v=VH84ppzmq9Q

4   Bollinger Bands

Bollinger Bands have been proven useful for traders. In theory, the stock is traded between the upper band and the lower band forming an envelope. For more info, click the following link.

http://www.investopedia.com/terms/b/bollingerbands.asp
https://www.youtube.com/watch?v=wfPf-KBuQH0

The following chart was drawn by Yahoo!Finance for CSCO from 8/7/2012 to 8/7/2014 selecting Bollinger Bands for the 50 days as a parameter. If you trade more often, use 20 days. If the chart is too small to display on your screen, enter the following in your PC's browser.
http://ebmyth.blogspot.com/2014/08/screen-csco-bollinger-bands-50.html

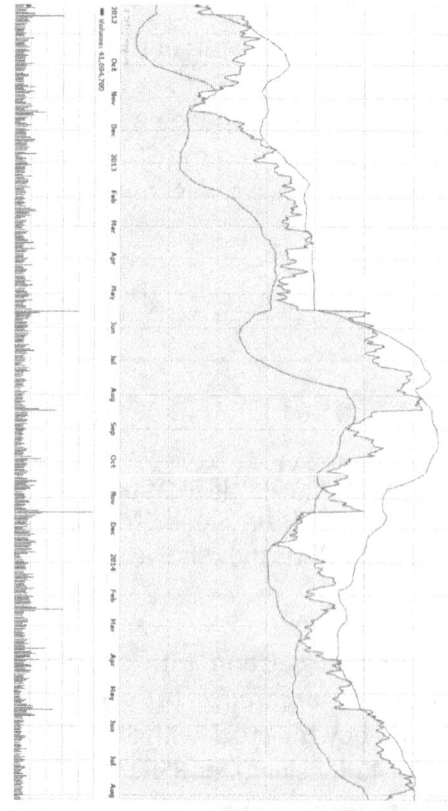

Bollinger Bands 50 Days.   Source: Yahoo!Finance

You buy the stock when the price is close to the lower band and sell the stock when it is close to the upper band.

When the stock price passes the upper band, it is called a breakout. Similar for the stock falling below the lower band. From the above, we should make some good money.

It is advisable to use at least one more technical indicator. I recommend the RSI(14), which is also accessible from Yahoo!Finance or similar sites. When it is above 70, it is overbought, so I recommend selling the stock. When it is below 30, it is oversold, so I recommend buying the stock. However, fundamentals have not been considered. Some stocks just go to zero and some just surge.

5 MACD

MACD, Moving Average Convergence Divergence, is an effective momentum (i.e., short-term) indicator used by most traders. When the stock price is crossing above the zero line, it is a buy and vice versa. It may give false signals in sideways fluctuation.
###
Again, try to master SMA and RSI(14) first. Using too many indicators usually harms you more than helps you. You can use Finviz.com to search stocks with technical indicators.

A TA strategy

Buy the stock, sector or the market when: 1. The SMA-50% (from Finviz) is above SMA-200%, 2. SMA-200% is positive, and 3. The price is at least 25% above the 52-week low (i.e., do not buy at the bottom as it may stay there for a long while). Sell, vice versa. Consider other metrics such as Volume, P/E, Debt / Equity, etc. It is great in concept, but I have not been convinced so far in my recent tests.
Related YouTube: Shorter Trend
https://www.youtube.com/watch?v=GAH9EyydEsM
Finding breakout stocks using Finviz.
https://www.youtube.com/watch?v=bWpe30R2VnM
Picking bottom: https://www.youtube.com/watch?v=ygjOTPqmRK4
A TA strategy: https://www.youtube.com/watch?v=ygjOTPqmRK4
Another strategy: CCI + MA

https://school.stockcharts.com/doku.php?id=technical_indicators:
commodity_channel_index_cci
https://www.youtube.com/watch?v=CuWzDo72-Rk

6   Other TA indicators/patterns

They are briefly mentioned here. Click on the links or use
Investopedia for more descriptions.

Double Bottom is a bullish pattern as the support line is stronger
than the resistance line.
Double Top is the opposite and is a bearish pattern. I prefer the price
of the second top is less than the price of the first top. It seems there
is no enough investment in this stock to break out of the second top.

Resistance and Support. The stock is supposed to fluctuate between
an imaginary zone of resistance and support. Short-term traders
may sell when the price is close to the resistance line and close any
short positions when it is close to the support line. However,
breakouts from this zone are possible and many traders trade stocks
on breakouts. It is a little similar to 52-week highs and lows. The
trend line indicates the trend of the stock.

Cup and handle is a bullish pattern. The stock price peaks and then
forms a shape of a cup and handle.

Head & Shoulder is a bearish pattern while the reversed Head &
Shoulder is a bullish pattern. It signals that the peak (the head) has

been reached and the second top (the shoulder) has failed to reach the previous peak.

Stochastic Oscillator. It is similar to RSI(14). Many traders use this indicator. If it is above 65, it is overbought. If it is below 30, it is oversold. In general, I would trade on an uptrend when the stock is moving from 60 to 85; it depends on how volatile the stock is. It is better to use with other indicators and as a reference.

To illustrate when to buy, one suggestion is to buy when this indicator changes to an uptrend while the price is still going down.

Many traders follow these technical indicators and SMA. They could become "self-fulfilled" prophecies.

Link

Chart patterns. https://www.youtube.com/watch?v=o6hZma0bajE
More: https://www.youtube.com/watch?v=aRlWle9smww
Resistance: https://www.youtube.com/watch?v=C2qRW9_via4

7   More on technical analysis

This chapter describes some TA indicators that can help us. Click on the following links for a better description.

- Finviz.com.
  It has SMA20%, SMA50% and SMA200% to represent the short-term, intermediate-term and the long-term indicator. SMA stands for Simple Moving Average and n for days for the duration of the average (for example, 20 days for SMA20%).

  If you are a long-term investor, use SMA-200% (or SMA-350%). Using SMA-20% would cause a lot of sells / reentries, which costs more in trading fees.

  Buy when the price is above the Moving Average line and sell when the price is below it. Finviz.com provides the percent of moving above the moving average to indicate just how much the price deviates from the average.

If you hold the stock for an average of 50 days, use SMA50%, and so on. If you hold stocks for an average of 90 days, you have to create your own SMA using one of the many websites including Yahoo!Finance and specify 90 days for the period.

Try other similar technical indicators such as EMA, which is supposed to weigh more on the more recent data. A weather man can predict tomorrow's weather better than the weather a week away.

- RSI(14) indicates whether the stock is overbought or oversold. RSI oscillates between zero and 100. Traditionally, and according to Wilder (the author of this method), RSI is considered overbought with a value above 70 and oversold with a value below 30 as described in the article.

  When it is oversold, most likely the stock will fall, and vice versa.

(http://stockcharts.com/school/doku.php?id=chart_school:technical_indicators:relative_strength_index_rsi)

Click here for another article. (http://financial-dictionary.thefreedictionary.com/Relative+Strength+Index)

- Cup and handle is a popular indicator of when the stock price would surge. (http://www.investopedia.com/terms/c/cupandhandle.asp)

- Double bottom indicates that the stock will move up. (http://stockcharts.com/school/doku.php?id=chart_school:chart_analysis:chart_patterns:double_bottom_revers)

  It shows a double bottom for Apple in 2013.

- A trading strategy: https://www.youtube.com/watch?v=asDBegQaupM

8   Using Fidelity

Click "Research and News" and then "Stock". Simple charting and advanced charting are both provided.

Hints:

- Fidelity provides suggested stops.
- Click on the Support and Resistance under Technical Analysis to display the Resistance Line (upper limit). Click on the Resistance Line and you can get the Support Line (lower limit).
- Click on Advanced Chart and then click on "learn how to use the chart".
- Under Advanced Chart, select Draw and Trend Line. Select the upper line by touching the highest points and do the same for the lower line.

#Filler: Future jobs
American blue-collar workers are facing a hard time for sure from driverless cars/trucks to robots. The future is also bleak for many professionals such as financial advisors, accountants, pharmacists...due to AI and cheap computing. The future will be owned by stock owners and the middle class will have jobs to make devices / software to remove jobs of the above workers. It may happen in our children or grandchildren's generation, and we can see it from above or below depending on what we did in life. LOL.

My daughter's first job was working for a company digitizing court cases for lawyers. In a minute or two, all the similar cases would be displayed. In the near future, AI would help to determine the chance of winning and summarize the arguments. In the not too long future, AI would represent the client to go to court and bill the client. Most likely, the judge would be a robot too.

9   Determine the exit point

I have described 2 exit strategies: Death Cross and SMA-350 (or SMA-400 for fewer false alarms). This is a bonus technique used stand alone or together with the above two. The concept is simple, but it requires more understanding on the charting and candlestick. All the three techniques can be applied to individual stocks, sectors and the market. We demonstrate it with the market using SPY, and the reentry point is just the opposite.

All the three techniques do not identify the top and the bottom as they are based on past data. However, it tells you to exit to avoid further losses. All three have false alarms, but this one could exit earlier. We can tune all the techniques to have fewer false alarms, but it would increase more losses than the original techniques.

The institutional investors (mutual funds, pension funds, etc.) move the market. That's why the volume is important. Whenever there is high volume, most likely they are trading seriously. They may want to make the market rosier than it really is by buying, but the volume is small. When they sell a lot, most likely the market will be down for a while. The following signals that the institutional investors are selling with the exception of the option expiration dates (the Friday of the third week in March, June, September and December):

- Today's trade session is unprofitable.
- The last trade session was unprofitable or had a very tiny profit.
- The trade volume is higher than the trade volume of the last trade session; candlesticks and trade volume are available from most charts.
- The trade volume is higher than the average trade volume of the last 50 trade sessions (available from most charts).
- If the above happens more often (such as 4 times in the last month), be careful. Due to the huge number of stocks the institutional investors own, they cannot sell them fast; I estimate it takes about 2 to 4 weeks to dump the stocks.
- The market falls for no reason; the only logical reason could be the institutional investors are dumping.
- Big fall before the market open and it continues for the entire trade day. It indicates many smart moneys including the retail investors are moving out of the market.
- Most likely, Death Cross and SMA-350 (or SMA-400) would signal a down market. SMA-200 would give you a signal ahead of the described two. Using SMA-50 and SMA-200:
  https://www.youtube.com/watch?v=BaZxE12cZP4&t=218s
  https://www.youtube.com/watch?v=wMxj6iB92ZA

Bonus: Miscellaneous

By the time you read this book, the current events may not be that current. Use the lessons to predict the future events.

1   Economy theories

I read this article predicting the "End of the economic cycle".
https://seekingalpha.com/article/4253126-weighing-week-ahead-near-end-economic-cycle?v=1554645177&comments=show

Why most market predictions by economists are wrong

It is interesting. The market cycle usually is 6 months ahead of the economic cycle. Based on this, the 'end' argument does not hold true. However, as of 4/09/2019, the market fundamentals are bad. I would move more to CDs after the settling of the trade war with China. To be warned, all markets are different.

I have about 10 hints for a potential market crash. The most deciding factor for me is the SMA, Simple Moving Average. When it turns negative, it is time to exit the market. The number of days in SMA depends on your risk tolerance. It is described in my book "Profit from coming market crash". SMA does not pinpoint the market peaks / bottoms as it depends on past data.

Most economists are wrong in predicting the market. The former Fed chairman said the economy was great and after a few months in 2008 the market crashed. There are many other factors such as politics and geopolitics. To illustrate, if there is a major war in the Middle East, the market would tank no matter how good the economy is.

The good job report is good for the economy as it would reduce the chance of a recession. However, if it is too good, the Fed would raise interest rates to cool down the over-heated economy and hence it would reduce corporate profits. Historically the market usually responds unfavorably to extreme low unemployment reports

The job report on April, 2019 is fine for both the economy and the stock market. However, mathematically incorrect, it is close to a practical zero unemployment.

Grouping world's economies

The world's leading economies are US/EU (with Canada and Australia) and the challengers are Japan, S. Korea and China in the last two decades. The first group's success is due to technology starting in the Industrial Revolution in Britain. The U.S. joined the group after WW2 when Europe was destroyed.

Eliminating resource-rich countries and small countries, we have about 25 countries leading the global economies. There are no strict rules on how to define a leading country. Most use GDP. I use GDP per capita adjusted for purchase power. U.S.'s GNP is higher than GDP as she owns a lot of foreign investments. China may not be counted as one by GDP per capita alone. However, China is the #2 economy due to its huge population and will be within the coming decade I expect.

The first group is declining slowly and is being replaced by the second group. It will take decades to be totally replaced judging from the decline of Spain and Italy which is described next.

In 1850s, Spain and Italy were the richest countries with the 'loots' from South American and other colonies. When the country is rich, the citizens want to enjoy life by asking for higher salaries, more vacation days, better social welfare, more protection for the workers and the environment. Hence, they lack the incentive to work harder and their products are less competitive. Are the U.S. and the EU countries repeating history?

The other factor is population size. Populations in most of the mentioned countries are shrinking. Aging population makes the problem worse. You need more educated and productive citizens. They solve part of the problem by immigration. EU is learning the hard way from many incidents caused by terrorists from immigration. The U.S. needs to immigrate top scientists to make us more competitive and the workers who are taking farm jobs and jobs not wanted by the social welfare recipients.

Most of these countries are borrowing heavily – a common trick by politicians in buying votes. It solves the current problems and buys some votes, but it will be a big burden for next generations. Watch out when the national debt is about twice the GDP. Japan has the lost decades. We and many EU countries have not learned from Japan. China has the same problem now. In addition, China's population has been surprisingly reduced even with the new two-child policy.

Most countries not included in the two groups will remain poor for decades to come. Many countries in Africa and S. America have high fertility rates. They may consume all the limited resources.

Most countries in the second group of the advanced economies are influenced by Confucius who teaches them to serve man and their family (actually the emperor to be precise). Confucius teaches them to be frugal (saving money for investing) and better educated for innovation.

It could be the climate too. Folks in the north have to work hard to prepare and save food for the winter. In warm climates, folks are lazier as described in my Coconut Theory. It does not explain why Australians are wealthy.

Another factor is life style. Many countries not included in the two group enjoy their life style by not chasing material stuff. They are happy by singing and dancing without fancy smart phones. Lack of consumption of fancy products would not make them an advanced economy. Good or bad? You decide. That's one reason Mao's era was backward as they're not chasing satisfaction from these consumers' products.

Globalization

During Reagan's era, globalization was preached and practiced. You do not want to grow sugar cane in Alaska. With the reduced cost of transportation and cheap labor in many countries, globalization has more benefits than drawbacks.

Many of our global companies have been making profits and GM may be saved from the second bankruptcy with the profits from China. We can find many U.S. fast food chains, U.S. movies and music and retail stores all over the world even in China.

The drawbacks are numerous. One major one is our huge trade deficit with China as she becomes the manufacturing capital of the world. As a result we have been losing a lot of factory jobs. The major drawbacks in China are both the air and water pollution. The other drawbacks are the lack of selection of products as price always favors over value for most consumers.

Both countries are addressing the problems. China will be more aligned with EU if she is being punished by us. China will buy more jets from Airbus than Boeing.

GDP and global trades

GDP normally means GDP growth after inflation.

Inflation is important. If the inflation is 10%, the GDP of 10 without including inflation is actually GDP of 0.

If the GDP is calculated in the U.S. currency, the currency conversion rate is important.

The average GDP for developing countries is about 5.5% and that for developed countries like the U.S. is about 3%.

China was about 6.2% in 2018. It is not a fully developed country. It used to be around 10 digits for many years after joining WTO in 2001. It is down from 2017's 6.9%. I predict it will be down below 6% if the trade war with the U.S. continues.

WTO rules have not been enforced fully on China esp. on subsidies and exporting their excessive capacity (product dumping for some). Most countries subsidized in some of their industries. Product dumping will in theory benefit the importing countries. We make sure that they will not raise prices after the local competitors have been driven out of business. Microsoft did dump their Office products one time. In addition, Microsoft and Apple copied many ideas from PARC.

China's GDP depends on the GDPs reported from the provinces. Most likely most provinces over-reported their GDPs.

Absolute GDP takes a back seat to GDP growth. The Debt / Absolute GDP ratio is important. Absolute GDP per capita is important when a living standard is concerned.

China is #1 in global trade. China owns less farm land and many natural resources such as oil per capita. China can use her trading position for political gains. During the current trade war with the U.S., Australia who is siding with the U.S. would lose a lot of Australia imports to China.

#Filler: Objectives in life

There are more important objectives in life than seeking wealth such as happiness, health, relationship... With wealth, a wise man can make the other objectives easier to obtain but an unwise man can do the opposite. When you lose a lot of money, you're still smiling then you're a winner.

My friend's friend died of worrying about losing most of his life saving in the stock market. Eventually the market returned, but he was dead already. We have to be emotionally detached to our wealth.

2   Actions to fix our problems

1. We consume more than we produce. Cut down on consumption, applied to both citizens and government. Our false prosperity depends too much on consumer spending. It has created all imbalances including a Federal deficit and trade deficit.

    Raising the interest rates would reduce consumer loans and investment loans at the expense of the stock market, building industry and big-ticket sales. We have to bite the bullet before it is too late.

2. We borrow more than we save. U.S. citizens save about 2% while Chinese save about 15%. Save more and do not max out your credit cards. We cannot postpone our debts to the next generations. Once-the-richest country borrows from the once-poorest country to support our spending.

3. We are not as competitive as we were in the 50s and 60s. Do not give out money generously to foreign countries. It made sense in the old days, but not anymore while EU, Japan, Israel and many have about the same wealth as us. When the government spends more in paying dividends on our gigantic national debts, we have less money to invest in infrastructure, education... that are important to boost our competitive edge.

4. The expenses of endless wars should go to investment for our future such as infrastructure.

    We no longer depend on oil from the Middle East, so we do not need to use military force to protect our oil route.

    Does Vietnam being a communist country today threaten us?

    We need to concentrate on cyber security. The lack of it would collapse our financial systems and expose our secrets / technologies.

5. The world is more competitive (esp. China) and it looks like it is getting worse. We can do better negotiations with our trade partners. The trade war is not the solution but taking out trade

barriers to our products is. We have to understand why we are not competitive. However, doing too much and too fast could lead to a global recession.

6. We need to give up some sectors such as those that are labor-intensive and/or environmentally harmful, and evaluate the benefits and losses.

7. We need to motivate our able welfare recipients to work to take up the jobs currently performed by illegal aliens. Our generous welfare system encourages folks not to work. If they work, they would lose all the subsidies. They are lazy but not stupid.

8. We need MORE (not less) H-1B visas to attract top scientists, engineers… to remain to have a competitive edge. However, only let immediate children come. Many of their parents come here and collect welfare to further burden our entitlement system.

   We also need international collaboration, relax restrictions on science research such as those in stem cells and promote starting new enterprises. Government should fund basic research. That's what we were leading the world in science and technology. China will eclipse us just in a matter of time if we do not think long term and take corrective actions now!

9. We need to balance the budgets, cut down entitlements, rebuild our school system, fund research, fund infrastructure (including security to protect our IP)…

   Make our broken health care delivery efficient.

10. We need to be doers instead of talkers. While we talked about the high speed rail (HSR) in California (that may not be useful here), China has over 60% of the global HSR. To start with, get the two parties to work together more. They disagree frequently with each other if the idea has not come from their own party.

11. Our children cannot compete with the Chinese, Japanese and Koreans. They spend too much time just enjoying life. If you believe they will achieve the same in life, you believe in fairy tales. Education starts at home. When we have too many single

parent families and teenage mothers, where is our future? We need to protect our youth from shootings, strong drugs and violence.

We need to bring back discipline and strong work ethics. The school must be a place to learn. Have we learned from too many shootings? We have to love our children more than our guns.

12. The military might should be supported by a strong economy but not in our case. If we were a company, we have been bankrupt with debts and entitlements. We have to put our priority and effort in improving our economy and be competitive.

Stop blaming others especially China for our problems that the politicians fail to fix. I blame the corporations on giving up our jobs and secrets to many countries including China in order to access their huge market and save on labor costs.

Realistically, most of the proposals above cannot be executed by politicians. They are more long- term solutions that the politicians are not interested in. The voters want to have the maximum benefits with the least taxes. We are a nation of free loaders unfortunately.

We are still leading the world in many sectors. We still have top-notch universities and profitable multi-national corporations. Do not live in denial and that we are not declining. Check out any top-notch college or any big high-tech corporation, you can find many foreign faces compared to 30 years ago. Most are new immigrants and their children.

It is hard for the leader of the global world to be humble. Our arrogance prevents us from collaborating with the rest of the world. If we can learn from our competitors and/or enemies, we could reverse the trend of our decline.

We may be following the footsteps of the great British Empire. Our technology revolution since WW2 may collapse like the British Industrial Revolution. Our reserve currency could follow the British pound in losing the status. Hopefully we will make corrections to reverse the trend. If the trend does not reverse, hopefully it is not in our life time.

3   Future trends

We're at the cross roads in many areas. Let me outline some of my thoughts. Check it out in five years and see how many have materialized.

Economy

1. Today the market is fundamentally unsound but technically sound. When technical goes down, it could be the time to exit the market.
2. FAANG as a group of stocks is very risky it seems to me. Netflix is the riskiest fundamentally.
3. Oil prices will take a break before its upward trend. When the oil price was at $30, I bought some oil stocks. When the oil price was at $50, I sold most of these oil stocks. I expected there to be fierce correction and at that time most sectors including oil would go down. Why did I expect an uptrend on oil after that? It is a simple supply and demand at work. Today drilling, exploration... are not economically feasible. Hence we should have less oil in the future and oil is still competitive and environmentally friendly.
4. China's "One Belt, One Road" Initiative will have impact on the world economy. It will benefit the participating countries and provinces in west China. Even many American companies including GE and Caterpillar will benefit by providing heavy equipment that China does not build today.
5. The world should benefit from the rise of China if China does not create wars.
6. From my estimate, only one job will be gained from 10 returned jobs from Mexico and China due to automation.
7. The wealth gap will be widened due to robots and the advance of artificial intelligence. It could have the biggest impact since the internet.
8. Europe will finally recover despite the rising of terrorism.

U.S.

1. The U.S. is declining but we're still leading in many sectors. We spend too much effort in being a world policeman while China is concentrating their efforts in improving the economy.
2. Trump may not be re-elected. Will it be the trigger to bring down the market? Only time can tell.
3. We used to be a nation of problem solvers, but have become people avoiding problems. Trump did that by dissolving his committee of business leaders. So is Yahoo!Finance. I miss many nice features from this site that are no longer available.
4. We need the H-1B program to attract the world's best programmers and scientists to make us more competitive. We need to monitor and enforce the program to ensure more benefits than harms.

4   Coming decades

The aging population, technology advances and China are major factors affecting the stock market today and specific sectors for the coming decades. These sectors may not rise or fall in a straight line.

The aging population is due to the baby boom after WW2. It is happening now. It gives rise to health care and medicines tailored to the growing needs. The seniors are supposed to withdraw their savings and then the market could tank. However, the market has been rising for the last 10 years and the drug companies are not doing as well in 2018. The population is rising fast in developing countries such as in Africa and India where the GDPs are low.

Technology such as robots and artificial intelligence will make many jobs obsolete. The internet could make newspapers obsolete as the readers can find articles that are free. If they do not adapt, they will perish. So are brick-and-mortar retailers to some extent. Most big chains have on-line stores. Mobile pay could replace credit cards.

When more electric cars are manufactured, gasoline prices would be reduced and many gasoline stations will have battery chargers replacing some gas pumps.

5G technology would make some sectors prospering while some become obsolete. Driver-less cars would be one that can benefit. After 2030, China will be the main force in a global economy. It has been slowed down by the trade wars of 2019.

5   Trading by headlines

On 6/29/2019, Trump and Xi seemed to settle trade war in the G20. The market would likely rise on the coming Monday. Luckily I had closed a short position. Many chip stocks would rise as they can sell their products to Huawei. I have several of these stocks expecting the trade war would be settled. The farmers and their supporting industry would breathe easier.

I bet the shipping companies would be more profitable from the news. Without doing further research, I checked out this shipping sector and found the following stocks had been up more than 4%: DHT, NM, SBLK, STNG, TNK and ASC. It was during the weekend, so your trade account should be able to trade after hours and you need to act right after the news.

I exchanged comments with Andrew McElroy, a sector rotation expert. He does not have the rules set up as in this book but he makes great trades by 'seeing' the market and using technical analysis. The following is from his article.

"The idea is fairly simple. There is more potential for profit (and loss) in individual sectors, especially when the index is trading sideways. I try to buy strong sectors which have pulled back onto support and avoid overbought sectors at resistance. I also use Elliott Wave to identify cycles of buying and selling and stages in trends."

I would like to include headlines such as Trump's election, interest rates hikes and new regulations.

When it rains in Brazil, buy coffee futures

Recently it rained too much in SE Asia, so buy rice futures. I did not trade futures, so I missed out on the opportunity and unfortunately there is no equivalent ETF for rice. In the beginning of 2012, we should know the farming crops especially corn will not be good due to the flooding and drought in different parts of the world. Act accordingly for the profit potentials.

When a war is starting in the Middle East, most likely the oil price will rise. Buy the oil ETF and sell it when the chance of the war is reduced. Many tiny drops of profit could turn into a river of profit.

Trading by headlines is profitable, but it is hard to master and is very time-consuming. Test this strategy on paper for years before you commit real money as in most strategies. Most couch potatoes read the newspaper and watch TV all day long without making a penny. He could be couch potato millionaire if he read this article, paper traded/refined the strategy and acted on it!

However, the media tend to exaggerate headlines in order to sell their ads. Ignore all the recommendations on stocks. Most likely they are outdated information and some may be used to manipulate others. Do your own research as your mother taught you that there is no free lunch.

Rules of the game

1. Do not be too emotional; ignore your past wins and losses except when using them as lessons if they are valid (i.e. educated guesses).

2. Do not trade the entire farm. Consider option, ETFs and/or small trade on stocks, which have too many other factors to be considered.

3. Trade it fast – today's headlines will not be headlines tomorrow. There are very few exceptions.

4. Where there is a winner, there is always a loser. For example, Apple was a winner with the iPhone and BlackBerry was a loser. Same for Best Buy and Circuit City.

5. Ensure you can trade after hours from your broker.

6. Do not forget when to exit for either a small profit or a small loss.

7. Quick evaluation. The headline will be gone if you do not act fast. Skip companies with poor metrics such as high debt and low earnings yield. Prefer to buy an ETF related to the headline.

8. Most likely someone has used the information before you get it. However, some info can be deducted before it occurs. Insider purchases is a good guide.

9. I recommended crude oil at $30 per barrel in Jan. 15, 2016 as the price was at rock bottom. For value sectors, you may have to wait for a long time for the market to realize its value.

10. Sometimes you ignore stock evaluations as the headline news is more important. Learn my 5-minute evaluation process of a stock (a quick way but not recommended if you have time to do thorough research):
   - From Finviz.com, enter the stock or ETF symbol. Look at how many greens in metrics over reds.
   - Check out Forward P/E (E>0 and P/E < 20), Debut / Equity (< 50%) and P/FCF (not in red color).
   - SMA20 (or SMA50 for longer holding period). If SMA20 is > 10%, it is trending up.
   - Scroll down for Insider Trade. It usually is a good buy if insiders are buying recently and heavily with market prices.
   - Be cautious on foreign and low-volume stocks.
   - If most of the above are positive, it is likely a buy. As in life, nothing is 100% certain.

If you have a hard time following the above, most likely this strategy is not for you and it is better to return to your couch. No offense.

Volatile market and headlines

As of 7/2012 (2015 too and historically a positive market in a year right before the election), the market went sideways and was influenced by headlines. 2013 had been volatile with dips and surges influenced by daily news. The trend was up though. The Federal debt problem, EU crisis... had not been resolved. Every time we had good news, the market rose, and vice versa. In this market, buy on dips (3% down from last temporary peak) and sell on temporary surges (3% up from last temporary bottom). Some use 5% instead of 3% depending on one's risk tolerance.

Trend and calendar timing

Usually following the trend is better than ignoring it.

- Many retail investors want to get rid of the losers for year-end tax planning. Buy them at year-end and sell them early next year. In the year end of 2012, it acted the opposite as folks were selling their winners expecting a larger tax bite next year but that turned out to be false.

  This could be the reason for a sell-off of Apple in year-end of 2012 and it gave us a good entry point. To me, Apple's fundamentals were sound though the media said otherwise. In a few months, Apple became a value stock from a growth stock according to the press.

- Investors are not rational and follow the market blindly. The strategy 'Buy low and sell high' works.

- We have so much good news and bad news in the same year. Ensure the bad news will not extend to worse news. Timing is everything. Buy on bad news and sell on good news; it does not work when the market plunges.

- The media influences the market. Analyze their arguments. If they exaggerate them, do the opposite.

- Over-reaction to earnings missed or gained. When the company missed the earnings by 5%, there is a very good chance the stock will be down in a year, and vice versa. However, when it missed by 1% and the stock lost by 10%, it could be a buying opportunity, particularly when it was a temporary condition and the company is fundamentally sound.

- Buy the stock at dip when a solvable problem surfaces. Sell after the problem has been resolved. Ceiling debt is such a solvable problem and it is caused by politics. In the beginning of 2013, I mentioned that the debt problem had not been resolved and we would have this ceiling debt problem periodically until it will be eventually resolved.

Scheduled events

Some events are scheduled such as earnings announcements, unemployment reports, etc. Most likely educated guesses of the outcomes have already been circulated in the web.

The last five events on the Federal debt handling (using fancy names such as sequester and debt ceiling) were scheduled such as the government shutdown. They drove the market down by about an average of 5% each time. Sell before the event and buy back afterward. The Congress has cancelled these debt deadlines as of 1/2014.

Many sectors are impacted by events such as Trump's success in election, hikes of interest rates and trade wars.

Follow the institutional investors

They drive the market. When they see the sector is over-valued or the peak has been reached, they rotate sectors.

Use deduction

In 2014, China has a great harvest on wheat, corn and rice. China's population is #1 in the world and its middle class is growing. The farmers in the US will be hurt as they cannot export these products to their number one customer. Use the same logic to deduct that there will be problems in the companies that supply products and services to the farmers. They are combines, fertilizer companies and seed companies. It further translates into Deere, Potash, Monsanto and AGCO.

Due to increasing wealth in 2017, Chinese demanded more meat. It takes a lot of corn to produce one pound of meat and in turn corn needed fertilizers. Hence, you can expect the companies producing fertilizers will increase their profits.

Geopolitical crisis

Many times no action is the best action. It applies here. I had my experience in selling too many stocks via stops in 911. The market returned in a few days and I did not buy them back.

An analysis from Ned David Research covers 51 events from 1900 to 2014. My interpretation for actions: Trade the affected sector (via sector ETF) in the first few days and reverse the trade 2 months after. Many times it means the oil price and gold price would rise.

I bought SH (a contra ETF to SPY) in August, 2017 as August and September are statistically the worst months in addition to the high risk in the current market. It is expected to be sold on Nov. 1. The North Korea crisis did not do much to the market on the first day but the market (the S&P 500) lost 1.45% and the risky NASDAQ lost 2.13% (see my blog on FAANG) on the second day.

Caveat. Need to understand the crisis. If it would lead to World War 3, most sectors will not recover for a long while. Again, there is no sure thing in investing otherwise there would be no poor folks. However, educated guesses should materialize more often than not.

My experiences
- When the interest rates is expected to rise, plan on investments that are favorable to it and vice versa.
- On the same week, CROX lost almost 40% in one day. I bought some and made about 10% profit in a week. CROX's fundamentals were no good and it did have a history of a roller coaster ride in its stock price. After a year, I found out that I sold it too early as the stock price doubled. Better to buy a stock on its way up than down unless we identify that the bottom has been reached.
- I was on vacation while the second incident of the Boeing Max happened. Should have shorted the stock. In addition, Boeing's suppliers would suffer too similar to Apple's suppliers on Apple.

  https://www.barrons.com/articles/boeing-737-max-jet-production-cut-suppliers-stocks-51554499957?siteid=yhoof2&yptr=yahoo

- I missed applying the same trick to the rise of Apple when Apple announced its new iPod. I should at least buy the stocks of its part suppliers. I hope learn from this lesson and take advantage of future similar circumstances.

I missed the opportunity to buy uranium stocks. It should be bought after Japan's disaster. When Japan approved the reopening of nuclear reactors today, these stocks including CCJ, DNN, LEU, URRE, UEC, URZ, URG and UUUU surge. When China's new nuclear reactors are on-line, they will surge again.

- Experiences in early 2014.
  Recently and in a short time, I made a good profit on BBY and a tiny profit on TGT. Both were bought due to headlines.

6   Earnings season overreactions

AAII has some screens for stocks with pleasant earnings surprises and bad earnings surprises (Jan., April, July and Oct.). The pleasant surprise screen always beats the other screens from the last time I checked.

Zacks ranks stocks with positive earnings revisions. Their stocks have ranked #1 has an amazing average annual return of 26% according to them. In 2019, the performance of recent tests did not hold up that well.

As with all vendors, we should check their recent performance (say, the last 5 years). If the strategy is proven to be effective, more investors will follow and usually make it less effective.

It usually starts on the first two weeks after the ending of quarters (Dec., March, June and September) as indicated in the following link. http://www.investopedia.com/ask/answers/08/earnings-season.asp

My experience

Contrary to the conventional wisdom, I enjoy the negative surprises more. If the company has a reason to come back or its problem is only temporary, I buy the stock. Sometimes it takes a few months and sometimes even a year for the stock to come back. The strategy of 'Buying low and selling high' works more often than it does not. However, avoid the stocks that start their long-term plunge.

Missing expected earnings by 1% and causing the stock to drop by

10% is a buy to me. Heading to bankruptcy is a different story though.

My momentum strategy buys stocks with positive earnings revisions. I usually do not keep these stocks for over a month.

As of today (4/6/2016), the quarter earnings season is starting. This year I have worry about the earnings due to the strong USD. It would impact the earnings as about 40% (my rough estimate) of the incomes of global companies are from foreign countries. If we feel there will be more disappointments, we should short the stocks that are expected to have poor earnings.

My lesson

Take advantage of the irrational human reactions. Retail investors and institutional investors are both human beings. Fund managers have more pressure to sell a loser to keep their jobs. Retail investors usually sell after the big institutional investors. Try to find out whether it is just a sentimental reaction or the stock is going to fall further.

How to hedge your stocks from earning surprises

Stocks might have a wide swing after the earnings announcements. Hedge the unfavorable announcements by the following three methods:

1. Stop loss.
   Usually the swing is steeper than your stop price. When the price reaches or go below a specific price, it will be turned into a market sell order. Institutional investors usually unload the stocks faster than the retail investors, opposite of buying. However, their positions are huge. We can tell they are unloading (or loading) from the unusual high trading volumes of the stocks. Ensure that your trades are allowed after hours.

2. Option.
   It is like buying an insurance to protect your loss. Protect yourself from large losses as insurance is not cheap and smaller losses could be due to volatility.

3. **Earnings prediction.**
    They are also known as whispers or educated guesses. Zacks has a grading system.

    Also insiders know the earnings before their announcements. However, it is illegal to use this information before its announcement.

Earnings revisions will be available before the announcement and they would provide better guesses to the announcement. With today's dividend chasers, the announcement of dividends or its increase would boost the stock price.

Personally I do not do a lot to protect my stocks from earnings announcements. I have too many stocks. However, when we have evaluated the stocks correctly and monitor them regularly, we should have more pleasant surprises.

Profit from earnings surprises

The stock price usually rises on positive earnings surprises and falls otherwise. Sometimes they are not rational such as 1% miss in earnings that causes 10% loss in the stock price. In some rare cases, the positive earnings causes the stock to plunge as the investors expected better earnings even better than consensus. Here is the example of looking for finding stocks with positive earnings (you can profit by buying puts or shorting the stocks for stocks with negative earnings).

*   Find stocks that have earnings announcements next week or month. Sources are Finviz.com's screener and SeekingAlpha.
*   The screened stocks should fit some basic criteria. My criteria are: Market Cap > 200M, stock price > $2, average volume > 10,000 shares...
*   If you subscribe to Zacks, check out the earnings grade. Stocks with Grade 1 and Grade 2 deserve our time for further research.
*   If there are meaningful insiders' purchases, the chance of positive earnings are high.
*   A positive short-term trend (SMA-20% from Finviz.com) is a plus

- A positive short-term trend for the sector that stock belongs to is a plus. The sector can be represented by an ETF for that sector and use SMA-20%.
- Read articles on the stock for a qualitative analysis. Find these articles from many sources including SeekingAlpha. Today they have fewer articles for free.

Be warned that we do not expect all wins. When we achieve more than 50% wins, we should fare very well financially. When the market is falling or the earnings are expected to be poor, do not buy stocks except those that are fundamentally sound.

Take advantage of others' orders

1. Ensure your account can trade after hours.
2. Use Finviz.com to look for stocks announcing earnings this week. Prefer fundamentally sound stocks with a market cap great than 500 (100 for smaller stocks).
3. Check out earningswhispers.com. They have two estimates: the consensus and the one from this website. Write down the exact time too.
4. If you subscribe Zacks.com, use its rating too as a reference.
5. Be at least 15 minutes earlier than the announcement date and time.
6. Google the stock and EPS from Google News. Refresh the search every 2 minutes. Check related articles.
7. If it beats the estimates, buy it at least one penny less than the last trade price and sell it within a day or two. The logic is to take advantage of all those orders that have not considered earnings in a timely fashion. It does not always work.
8. To improve performance, include Revenue with EPS.

Personally I do not do it as it is too time-consuming for me; my beauty sleep is more important than money. Again test it out before committing real money. There are many parameters that can be tuned to adjust to your personal preferences and the current market conditions. This is the essence of an entire book. I read with my own enhancements such as using Finviz.com.

7   Selling short

This article describes the advantages, disadvantages and how to avoid the pitfalls in selling short. Next we describe the procedures.

Advantages

You consider short selling (same as shorting) when you believe the stock and / or the market is going down. It is easier to make money via selling short than buying stocks especially in a plunging market. Many mutual funds cannot short stocks, and consequently they spend less time in searching for poor companies. The other factor is psychology: Most retail investors do not want to sell losers.

You should start paper trading. Commit a small amount of money gradually when you have proved to yourself your strategy (i.e. what and when to short sell, and exit) is profitable. Consult your financial advisor first and read my Disclaimer under Introduction.

Beginners should try to short the sectors by buying contra ETFs. The major advantages are: 1. Less volatile, 2. Can trade in retirement accounts (some brokers have some restrictions), 3. Do not lose more than your initial trade position, and 4. Fees and dividends are handled for you. Short selling stocks is risker but more profitable than a group stocks in ETFs.

Disadvantages and some suggestions

- Short stocks when the market is plunging and limit your shorting positions when the market is rising. The market rises more than falls, and hence be careful. However, when the market plunges, it is fast and steep.

- Could lose more than 100% of the investment.
  Actually, in theory, there is no limit. If the price of the shorted stock rises by 10 times, the loss is well over 10 times the money of the short position. The 2015 example was Weight Watchers. The price boosted up by more than 170% when Oprah took out a position on them. Fundamentally this stock was not sound and it should be shorted. No stock pickers without insider information (that is illegal) can predict that. Use stops to protect

your trade (i.e. cover your short when you lose a percent specified by you).

- Need to pay dividends and interest for the shorted stock.
  The higher the dividend rate for the stock, the more you have to pay. Investors should avoid high-dividend stocks when shorting unless the expected shorting period is only brief.

  In addition, you need to pay interest for 'borrowing' the stocks to sell. Brokers charge interest rates differently and it could be huge savings to shop around if you short stocks a lot.

- Need both fundamental and technical analyses.
  From my experience, technical analysis is more important than fundamentals in shorting especially for short holding periods.

- If shorting a stock is successful and closed within a year, the gain is usually subjected to the short-term capital gains taxes which are typically higher than the long-term capital gains taxes. Check the current tax laws and consult your tax lawyer.

- Not all of the stocks can be shorted. Your broker may not have the stock you want to short. It is also possible that your broker can close out your short positions for various reasons; they need to protect their 'loans' to you. Check the margin status with your broker.

- Selling short is not allowed in retirement accounts as of 2020. However, you can buy contra ETFs for a group of stocks to bet against the market or a specific sector, but not on a specific stock in retirement accounts.

- The following sectors are riskier: the drug, mine, bank (unless you know the quality of their mortgages) and insurance sectors. An approval of a drug could drive the stock price up by more than 25% in one day. The same for earnings announcements. It could drive the stock more than 10% in either direction.

- Your screens may find many stocks in bio tech companies. These companies especially with a market cap of less than 1B may have the worst fundamentals. However, when they have a new discovery, the stock prices could rocket. Do not short them when insiders are buying (Insider Transaction on Finviz.com) and high SMA-20% or SMA-50% (from Finviz.com).

- There is no perfect timing. Some stocks fluctuate a lot with no rational reasons, or the prices are driven by institutional investors. Some stocks could be manipulated. The shorted stocks could move up for a long time until they finally crash. Hence, do not short against a rising stock, a sector or a market. When the market is rising, shorting a rising stock in a rising sector is dangerous, and the opposite could be profitable for shorting.

- The best time to short is when the market is plunging. At that time, the best sectors to short are those sectors that are plunging. Hence, find the worst stocks in a worst sector in a plunging market.

- A bad company could be acquired by another company due to a good buy; it could boost its stock price. It is same when the major problem of a company has been fixed.

- Use mental stops (i.e. set a price you can afford to lose and when it reaches the specific price, place a market trade to exit the shorted shares. You do not want to make 5% several times and lose 50% in one trade.

- You may not want to short companies that are fundamentally unsound but with a good momentum (i.e. trending up). They may have good prospects such as improved profit, being turned around, settling a lawsuit and/ or new products are being legalized and/or approved. If you do, then use mental stops to protect your trades.

- Never short sell the stocks that are rising even they are not fundamentally sound such as FAANG in 2015 to 2020. Tesla has gained many times and you have to pay the gains, not limited to your short position.

- I have turned some short selling candidates into buying due to the high insiders' buying and/or high short squeeze potential.

- Watch out for short squeezes when the short percentage approaches over 25%. In a nut shell, the stock is running out of shares to be shorted. As a result, it would rise in price especially on any good news. As of 8/2015, I expect short squeeze for PPC and SAFM (CALM in 12/2015) for the following reasons:

1   The shorting has no bases. It is most likely from one or two hedge funds.
2   Fundamentally sound.
3   Beef will be replaced by a lot of healthier and cheaper chicken if not already, esp. during the drought in California.
4   In Hong Kong for example, they do not allow live chickens imported from China during the bird flu breakout, but they did allow frozen chicken from the USA if there was no political game going on.

What to buy & how

Refer to the chapter on screening short candidates. If Fidelity's Equity Summary Score for the stock is below 4, it is a short candidate.

The following are my suggestions on shorting stocks that have the potential to go down. Basically these stocks are both fundamentally unsound and technically unsound. Many sites (some require paid subscriptions) provide a composite grade for fundamentals and technical. Finviz.com. a free financial site, does provide most of these metrics and many of them are discussed here. If you do not hold the shorts for a long period, technical (the trend) parameters are more important. Parameters for short candidates are:

- Fundamentals

  - The price is more than four times the book value.
  - EY (= 1 / (P/E) is negative. Negative PEG is another consideration.
  - High debts (Debt/Equity > .5) except for industries that require high debts such as utilities.
  - Insiders are unloading their company's stocks. They do this for many reasons. But, when they are buying, do not short

the stock as they may know some positive events that we do not know.

- Bad intangibles such as losing market share and/or a major lawsuit(s) is pending.

  Read articles on the company from Finviz, Fidelity, Seeking Alpha, etc.

- Do not short stocks that are on their uptrend. It includes the current marijuana stocks that most have no fundamental values and/or historical data.

- Do not short small stocks with a small market cap or float. I usually short stocks with a market cap or float > 200M (100M for riskier investors). Use higher values for conservative investors.

  The stocks with small floats may be controlled by the owners; if they do not sell, the stocks available to trade will be limited. Another indicator is the Avg. Daily Vol. Personally it should be 100 times higher than my bet.

- Technical metrics:

  - Be careful on stocks that have plunged more than 15% recently (Finviz's last quarter performance gives us some hint). It could mean the bottom has been reached.
  - Overbought (RSI(14) > 65). There may be a reason, so it is only a secondary consideration. Most stocks to be shorted may have RSI(14) less than 30.
  - The momentum metrics such as SMA-20 and SMA-50 are important too. SMA-20% and SMA-50% from Finviz.com should be negative (i.e. trending downwards).
  - Some sites especially the paid sites may give you a momentum grade. Select the stocks with a bad momentum grade (a.k.a. timing grade). However, if it is the lowest grade, be careful, as it has nowhere to go but up.

Trading considerations
- Do not trade in the first hour (first half hour for me) as there may have new developments overnight.
- I use subscription services. I do not trade on Monday or the day after a holiday, as the data is at least one day late.

- Your broker may limit your short trade (limited order) to be valid for the day; check this with your broker.
- Your broker may need to approve whether you can short stocks based on your experiences.
- When you sell short and are using limit orders, enter a sell price higher than the last trade price just like selling a stock.
- Close the short position when your trade loses a pre-defined percentage which depends on your personal tolerance.
- Put Option is similar to shorting a company. It is not for beginners.

Margin

Margin should not be used extensively. It is expensive and most brokers try every trick they can to squeeze profits from all transactions to subsidize their low-commission incomes. Usually you can borrow up to 40% of your current position and the rules and the margin rates vary among brokers.

Many investors had losses during the last two market plunges. However, many including myself had made a killing in 2003 and 2009 using margin. I use it for the following reasons.

- For convenience in placing buy orders that exceed my cash position in my taxable accounts.
- I can pay back my outstanding margin loans from my home equity loan (check the current tax laws) as it is far, far lower than my broker's margin interest rates. However, I do not recommend this for conservative investors.

Random case

- As of 7/2013, shorting Amazon, Netflix and Tesla as a group was not beneficial. It is best to stay away from shorting, except during the plunging (from peak to bottom) in the market cycle.
- Did you watch 60 minutes on Lumber Liquidators in 2015? That's how you do shorting. Find out why the company boosts its profit and stock price in such a short period. If it has been proven to be fishy, place a short position. However, when the news becomes public, it could be too late for us to act.

- As of 1/15/2015, GME had a short squeeze. The stock was up by 10% with a decent earnings announcement. I am surprised that the short % was over 45% for a decent stock with a decent P/E. It had low debts and decent cash reserves. The shorters (same as short sellers) must be losing their shirts. Even for the fundamentally sound Netflix and Tesla, the shorters (one by a famous hedge fund manager) would lose a fortune; Tesla was at one time 11 times its lowest price.

Links & Articles
Introduction
https://www.youtube.com/watch?v=oMnmTV5HF5Y&list=WL&index=3&t=605s

Tilson
Put Options.http://en.wikipedia.org/wiki/Put_option
Fidelity Video: Options.https://www.fidelity.com/learning-center/options/finding-options-strategies/options-analysis-tool-video
Fidelity Video: Selling short.https://www.fidelity.com/learning-center/trading/selling-short-video

Filler 12 noon is not 12 pm

The Chinese restaurant I went to says they are open at 12 am. Are they wrong or is the world wrong?

The next hour after 11 am is 12 am, NOT 12 pm. The one who set it up did it totally wrong and no one complains about it until now. If I were born earlier, I would have corrected it.

8   Simplest way to evaluate stocks

Beginners should trade ETFs only. This chapter is for the readers who are ready or getting ready to trade stocks. In general, ETFs are diversified, less volatile than trading stocks. However, stocks offer higher profit but higher risk.

Many stock researches have already been done recently and some are available free of charge. I have no affiliation with Fidelity except I retired from it. You can open an account with them with no balance. Their Equity Summary Score is one of the best indicators; I check out **value** stocks with score higher than 8. Concentrate on fundamental metrics such as P/E for long-term holds, and momentum metrics for short-term holds. Add criteria to limit the number of screened stocks. Finviz.com is a free screener.

Several sources

The popular ones are Morningstar, Value Line, The Street and Zacks (currently free for rankings of individual stocks). If they are not free, check out whether they are available from your local library. I have 3 simple ways to evaluate stocks starting with the simplest. In addition, read the articles on the selected stocks from Fidelity, Finviz, Seeking Alpha and many other sources for further evaluation.

Fidelity

Select only stocks that have Fidelity's Equity Summary Score 8 or higher. There are tons of information about a stock. Once a while I did not agree with the score such as SHOP and ZM that scored high in August, 2020. Include the following for your analysis.

A modified stock selection based on a magazine article

Most metrics are available from Finviz except EV/EBITDA.

1.   Forward P/E (expected earnings and not based on the last twelve months). It should range from 5 to 15 (10 to 25 for high tech stocks). EV/EBITDA (from Yahoo!Finance) is a better choice as it includes the debts and cash than P/E; it would be more effective if it uses forward earnings. If you do not use EV/EBITDA,

ensure Debt/Equity is less than 0.5 except for the debt-intensive industries.

2. ROE (Return of Equity) measures how well the company uses the capital. I prefer stocks with ROE greater than 5%.

3. Volatility. Conservative investors should select stocks with a beta of less than one (i.e. less volatile).

4. Insider Transactions for sales (i.e. negative) from should be less than 5%. If it is -5%, most likely the insiders are dumping it.

5. Compare the metrics such as P/E and Debt/Equity to its five-year average and its competitors (available in Fidelity).

6. Momentum. Check out the SMA-50 (actually SMA-50%) and SMA-200. Ideally they should be positive. SMA-50% is especially important for stocks you do not want to keep for a long time.

7. Check out articles on the stock as some recent events (for example a new lawsuit) have not been included in the metrics.

8. Compare the trend of the sector this stock is in. Under Finviz, enter the related sector ETF.

Summary
The sources are Fidelity (Equity Summary Score and various comparisons), Finviz and Yahoo!Finance (for EV/EBITDA). Value stocks should be held longer.

Category	Score / Metric	Value /Momentum
Score	Fidelity's Equity Summary Score	Both
Value	EV/EBITDA	Value
	P/E cheaper compared to 5-year avg.	Value
	P/E cheaper compared to its sector.	Value
	Insider Purchases	Both

Safety	Debt/Equity	Value
	Compare it to its sector.	Value
Momentum	50-SMA%	Momentum
	200-SMA% (for long term holds).	Value
Articles	Check out latest events	Both
Market	No purchase if market is risky.	Momentum

A simple scoring system using Finviz

Bring up Finviz.com and then enter the stock symbol.

No.	Metric	Good	Bad	Score
1	Forward P/E[1]	Between 2.5 and 12.5, Score = 2	> 50 or < 0, Score = -1	
2	P/ FCF[1]	< 12, Score = 1	>30 or < 0, Score = -1	
3	P/S[1]	< 0.8, Score = 1	< 0, Score = -1	
4	P/ B[1]	< 1, Score = 1	< 0, Score = -1	
	Compare quarter to quarter of last year			
5	Sales Q/Q	> 15%, Score = 1	< 0, Score = -1	
6	EPS Q/Q	> 20% , Score = 1	< 0, Score = -1	
			Grand Score	
	Stock Symbol Date[2]	Current Price	SPY	

Footnote

[1] Negative values for Sales (due to accounting adjustments), Equity and Book are possible but not likely.

[2] The last row is for your information only. SPY is used to measure whether it will beat the market by comparing the return of this stock to the return of SPY.

The Score

Score each metric and sum up all the scores giving the Grand Score. If the Grand Score is 3, the stock passes this scoring system. Even if it is a 2, it still deserves further analysis if you have time. You may want to add scores from other vendors. To illustrate on using Fidelity, add 1 to the score if Fidelity's Equity Summary score is 8 or higher. Monitor the performance after every 6 months or so to see whether this scoring system beats the market.

Very basic advice for beginners

Beginners should stick with U.S. stocks with Market Cap greater than 800 M (million), Debt/Equity less than .25 (25%) except for debt-intensive industries such as utilities and airlines and Forward P/E between 5 to 20 (25 for high-tech companies). These metrics are all available from Finviz.com, which is free.

Do not have more than 20% of your portfolio in one stock (unless it is an ETF or mutual fund) and do not have more than 30% of your portfolio in one sector.

For more conservative investors, buy non-volatile stocks whose beta (available from Yahoo!Finance) is less than 1. Beta of 1 represents the market (the S&P 500 index). For example, a stock with beta 1.5 statistically fluctuates more than 50% of the market and hence it is very volatile.

Try paper trading to check out your strategy and your skill in trading stocks. If your broker does not provide one, use a spreadsheet to record your trades or check the availability of simulator.investopedia.com.

#Filler: Silence is golden

I am glad I did not give advice to a friend who had to decide whether to take a lump sum payment or an annuity. The correction in March, 2020 would wipe out a lot of his portfolio if he took the lump sum payment. No one would share his profits when the predictions are correct, but the blame if it does not materialize.

It is same in investing that nothing is certain. With educated guesses, we should have more rights than wrongs especially in the long run.

9   Evaluating a sector

The following is for illustration only. The figures are from 12/20/2020 and the sector is "XLK", the technology sector.

Determining the trend

Bring up Finviz.com from your browser. Enter "XLK" for the ticker (stock symbol).

From the graph, it shows it is in an uptrend.

Most of us use SMA50 (Simple Moving Average for the last 50 sessions). It is 6%, and hence the ETF is up. SMA20 is for average holding period of the last 20 sessions, and is 3%. The percentage gives us how the average is above the current price.

My holding period is about 30 sessions and I use the average value. In this case it is about 4.5%. If you want to be more precise, you can open a chart and specify 30 sessions for SMA.

SMA200 is for long-term hold, and most of us do not care about it for short-term sector rotation.

Other parameters

RSI(14). If it is higher than 65, watch out for oversold condition, which could indicate a higher chance to reverse the trend. Some sectors just keep on rising. The best way is to use trailing stops (you update the stops every week or so from the current prices).

P/E. It is not available on Finviz.com. Bring up dbETF.com. From the Search icon, enter XLK. It indicates a P/E of 28.57. It is a better value than the average of most sectors; it ranks 18 out of 42. For Sector Rotation, value parameters such as P/E are not that important as the trend value.

Holdings. Click on Holdings in dbETF. This ETF is weighed by Market Cap and Apple is comprised of about 24% of the Assets. The next one is Microsoft with 19% of the Assets. It is quite risky, and not as diversified as expected. These two stocks is about 43% of the total Assets of this ETF. If you have $100,000 to invest, you can invest 24% of the $100,000 in Apple and 19% of $100,000 in Microsoft. In this way, you have better control and save the management fees.

Many parameters such as Finviz's Debt/Equity, Insiders' Transactions, Short%, Quarter-to-Quarter Sales and Profits can be estimated by making the proportional averages of these parameters of these two stocks.

Other parameters from dbETF

Technicals.

SMAs are available here. I prefer the percentages from Finviz.

Beta of 1.06 in this example indicates this ETF is more volatile than the average stock. MACD, Bollinger Brands, Supports / Resistance and Stochastic are available. They are useful, but you have to fully understand these technical parameters.

Intangibles

There are other considerations that affect the performance of the sector. Apple could be a victim of the trade war with China. There are many sectors that will be affected by today's pandemic. For example, in Feb, 2020, we should know the pandemic was coming. At that time, you should unloaded ETFs and stocks related to travel such as airlines and cruise lines if you had them. The riskier investors should consider shorting them. The excessive printing of money would give rise of ETFs related to gold and gold miners.

One strategy

Find the best sectors with best values (based on P/E for example) and select the top one or two best momentum ETFs as described here.
https://www.youtube.com/watch?v=uwfrdxxtULk&list=WL&index=112

Epilogue

Initially, I want to write a book for one reader only: Me. My children have better things to do than investing. I do not need to keep my 'secrets' for them. That's why I publish this book. From the version before its release, it had been doing better than my expectation. It has been very rewarding, when my readers tell me how much they enjoy and benefit from this book. I never forget the excitement I held my first paper back in my hands for the first time.

It is far more financially rewarding working on my investment including finding new strategies. Writing books and articles takes time away from my investing and it actually costs me more money. However, it has been fun to write this book and to interact with my readers. Money cannot buy everything.

I do not believe that this book or any book is the Holy Grail in investing.

There are two simple techniques: one with chart and one without. Both of them worked in the last two plunges. I discovered the trick after 2000 and found 350 days is the best fit.

In 2000, I read many articles including one that said "The conference room of an S&P 500 company can fit the entire company which has about the same market value". The low quality of the commercials in Super Bowl told us how incapable these CEOs were. One internet vendor gave me $50 for using their product and I would not spend $50 in my entire life for that product. Too many bad examples!

I had a hard time to convince my friends to exit the market from their huge returns. Some wanted to quit their jobs as their genius minds can make millions just working a few hours a week. It is impossible to ask the lottery winners not to buy lotteries.

In other words, these interest companies were far over-priced. I switched most if not all my tech holdings to traditional sectors in the first two weeks of April, 2000. It would be far better to cash.

They did not have contra ETFs then; anyway my broker firm did not allow me to short stocks. Even for that, it saved me a bundle.

In 2007, I was blinded by the big profits in my oil stocks and did not follow my chart. Not again and I require myself to be a reader too! The techniques are so simple and most likely they are not invented but only publicized by me.

This book represents my knowledge in market timing. If you do not put this knowledge into action, it will not do you any good. You should refine the techniques to suit your personal requirements and risk tolerance. Again, you are responsible for all the profits and losses. Hence, test it out to identify what works for you. Also the market is not always rational. Your investment decisions should be improved with a proven system than without but nothing is guaranteed in life.

If you're ultra conservative and/or do not want to do any charting, here is one suggestion.

When the SPY's SMA-200% (from finviz.com) is negative, take about 20% of your stocks off the market. Select those stocks that have the worst appreciation potential and/or risky. When the SMA-200% is negative by more than 10% (i.e. -10%), take another 30% off. When it is more than -15%, take the rest off the market.

The numbers are arbitrary and adjust them to your personal risk tolerance. Do the opposite in returning to the market. The beauty is you do not have to do any charting.

If you believe this book is beneficial, please comment in amazon.com or similar sites.

https://www.amazon.com/dp/1537509152

*** The End ***

Appendix 1 – All my books

- Art of Investing (highly recommended combining most of my books on investing). It has over 500 pages (6*9), double the size of an average investing book. Similar books: Using Fidelity. Using Finviz.
- Sector Rotation: 21 Strategies and Shorting Stocks and ETFs have more specific chapters on the topic.
- Using Profitable Investing Sites. Investing Lessons.
- Best stocks for 2022.
- "Nuclear War with China?"
- Books for today's market: Profit from Coming Market Crash.
- The following books are in a series: Finding Profitable Stocks, Market Timing and Scoring Stocks.
- Books on strategies: Trading System, Swing (Rotation + Momentum), ETF Rotation for Couch Potatoes, Momentum, SuperStocks, Dividend, Penny & Micro Stock, and Retiree.
- Books for advance beginners: Be an expert (highly recommended), Introduce, Investing for Beginners, Beat Fund Managers, Profit via ETFs, Buffett, Ideas, Conservative and Top-Down.
- Miscellaneous: Investing Strategies. Buy Low and Sell High. Buy High and sell Higher. Buffettology. Technical Analysis. Trading Stocks.
- Concise Editions and Introduction Editions are available at very low prices and are competitive with books of similar sizes (50 pages) and prices ($3 range).

Most books have paperbacks. Links and offers are subject to change without notice.

Best stocks to buy for 2022

We care about performance only. Not considering dividends and fees, my last three books in this series have beaten the SPY (the market to most) by **110%, 71% and 25%** from the publish date to 07/01/2021. Next book could be on 12/15/2022

Book	Stocks	Return	Ann.	Beat SPY by
Best Book for 2021 2nd Edition	10	20%	52%	110%
Best Book for 2021	4	29%	52%	71%

Best Book to Buy from Aug, 2020	14	42%	45%	25%
Avg.	9	31%	50%	69%

Sector Rotation: 21 Strategies

- On 5/26/2020, I searched for "Sector Rotation" under Amazon's Book. They are listed in the same order except my book Sector Rotation: 21 Strategies.

Book	Date	Size[1]	Kindle $[1]	Hard $
Sector Rotation: 21 Strategies	**05/2020**	**425**	**$9.95**	$24.95
Super Sectors	09/2010	289	$26.39	$49.95
Dual Momentum Investing	11/2014	240	$40.40	$42.20
Sector Investing	05/1996	260		$29.94
Sector Trading Strategies	08/2007	164	$26.39	$16.66
The Sector Strategist	03/2012	225	$26.39	$44.96
ETF Rotation	10/2012	125	**$9.95**	**$14.99**
Optimal... Sector Rotation	07/2015	80		$44.07

[1] From Amazon on size and prices as of 5/25/2020.

My book won in all categories except the price for hard copy in one. However, my book won as the lowest cost per page by a wide margin. In addition, as of 5/2020 I bet that no author besides me made over 4 times using sector rotation starting the amount more than his yearly salary then.

- I have **21** strategies in sector rotation while most books have only one. It ranges from simple rotation of a stock ETF and cash for beginners to many advanced strategies for experts. Most other books have one or two strategies.
- Andrew, a contributor on Sector Rotation article at Seeking Alpha, said, "Great stuff, Tony. It's great to meet experienced traders such as yourself. I had a browse through the book and think your method is a little more refined than mine."
- "You have written the book in a way that makes good and logical sense." Bill.
- Do not be fooled by past performances. Just check the recent performance of the top 50 stocks selected by IBD in the last five years. The mediocre result (hopefully it will change) could be due to too many followers and/or there is no evergreen strategy. I seldom heard the

fantastic results from the followers of O'Neil, our greatest chartist. The adaptive strategy of this book shows you how to select the most profitable strategy for the current market.

- I switched most (if not all) my sector funds in April, 2000 from technology sectors to traditional sectors (better to money market fund). We can reduce losses by spotting market plunges and the sector trend.

Shorting Stocks and ETFs

Recent performances.

Stocks	Short Date	Close date	Duration	Return	Annualized
ACVA	06/10/21	09/29/21	111	22%	72%
CCL	07/14/21	09/29/21	77	-8%	-36%
CENX	09/17/21	09/29/21	12	3%	105%
CLOV	09/16/21	09/29/21	13	10%	291%
CSPR	09/16/21	09/29/21	13	33%	917%
EOSE	09/15/21	09/29/21	14	10%	261%
MILE	07/22/21	09/29/21	69	53%	279%
NCLH	07/27/21	09/29/21	64	-5%	-27%
REAL	06/04/21	09/29/21	117	22%	68%
UAVS	06/04/21	09/29/21	117	41%	127%
Average	07/30/21	09/29/21	61	18%	206%
RSP	S&P 500			0%	

It is for education purposes and I am not responsible for any errors. As in most parts of this book, commissions, dividends and fees (interest for shorts) are not included, and hence the returns are less than specified. They are real and all trades for the period.

Stocks	Short Date	Close date	Duration	Return	Annualized
BBIG[1]	09/30/21	11/19/21[1]	50	35%	258%
BFLY	09/30/21	11/18/21	49	14%	107%
EOLS	11/10/21	11/17/21	7	10%	523%
FLDM	10/13/21	11/18/21	36	14%	147%
MKFG	10/27/21	11/18/21	22	-9%	-149%
PAVM[1]	10/20/21	11/19/21[1]	30	34%	413%
TSP	10/05/21	11/18/21	44	-11%	-91%
VRM	10/13/21	11/17/21	35	13%	135%
Average	10/14/21	11/18/21	34	13%	168%
RSP	S&P 500			4%	

Appendix 2 – Art of Investing

Art of Investing consisting of 15 books in 1. Besides saving money and your digital shelve space, it gives you quick reference and concentration on the topic you're currently interested in. It covers most investing topics in investing excluding speculative investing such as currency trading and day trading. It has over 500 pages (6*9), about the size of two investing books of average size.

The 15 books

Book No.	Amazon.com
1	Simple techniques
2	Finding Stocks
3	Evaluating Stocks
4	Scoring Stocks
5	Trading Stocks
6	Market Timing
7	Strategies
8	Sector Rotation
9	Insider Trading
10	Penny Stocks & Micro Cap
11	Momentum Investing
12	Dividend Investing
13	Technical Analysis
14	Investing Ideas

15	Buffettology

The book links are subject to change without notice.

"How to be a billionaire" is for beginners and couch potatoes, who can use the advanced features of this book in the simplest and less time-consuming techniques. Most advance users can skip this section unless they want to use some of the short cuts described.

We start with the basic books Finding Stocks, Evaluate Stocks, Trading Stocks and Market Timing. You can select and start with one of the many styles and strategies in investing such as swing trading and top-down strategy. Many tools are described in other books such as ETFs, technical analysis, covered calls and trading plan.

Many books start with "Why" to lure you to read more and are followed by "How" and then the theory behind the book.
If the book you're reading is beneficial to you, imagine how it would with 850 pages.

Most readers' comments are on "Debunk the Myths in Investing", which this book is originally based on. As of 2018, I did not know any of the commentators on my books.

"I skipped ahead to his chapter book 14 (of "Complete the Art of Investing"), Investment Advice just to get a feel of his writing style. His research is phenomenal and doesn't overwhelm with big words or catchy "sales-like" tactics.

I truly believe this ordinary man, Mr. Tony Pow, has a gift of explaining his experience as an investor without the bull crap of trying to make you buy his stuff. He seemingly just wants to share his knowledge, tips, and clarity of definitions for the kind of folks like me who want to understand something FIRST before jumping in with emotions of trying to make a boat load of money. I like the technical analysis side he brings.

Mr. Tony Pow talks about hidden gems in his book; well....quite frankly, he is a hidden gem. Thank you and I will also post my comments about this author to my Facebook page!" – JB on this book.

"Excellent book, recommend to all investors... great knowledge. It has fine-tuned my investing strategies... Your book is hard to set aside, as I read it all the time learning good techniques and analysis of stocks, ETF... Since I purchased your book in March, I have underlined, highlighted and placed tabs on top of pages for quick reference." – Aileron on this book.

"Tony, I just finished reading your 2nd edition. It's my pleasure to report that I found it most interesting. You're welcome to use this blurb if you like:

Debunk the Myths in Investing is an all-encompassing look at not only the most salient factors influencing markets and investors, but also a from-the-trenches look at many of the misconceptions and mistakes too many investors make. Reading this book may save not only time and aggravation but money as well!"

Joseph Shaefer, CEO, Stanford Wealth Management LLC.

"Tony, Great work!" from James and Chris, who are portfolio managers.

"'Debunk the Myths in Investing' is a comprehensive book on investing that deals with many aspects of this tense profession in which with a lot of knowledge and a bit of luck (or vice versa) one can greatly benefit...

Therefore 'Debunk the Myths in Investing' is an interesting book that on its 500 pages offer a lot of knowledge related to investing world and many practical advice, so I can recommend its reading if you're interested in this topic."
- Denis Vukosav, Top 500 Reviewers at Amazon.com.

"490 pages (Debunk) of a genius's ranting and hypothesis with various theories throughout, written light-heartedly with ample doses of humor...Yes, the myth of not being able to profitably time the market is BUSTED...

One might ask... Why is he giving away the results of his hard-earned research for only $20? He states that his children are not interested in investing and wants to share his efforts with the world." - Abe Agoda.

"Excellent book, recommend to all investors... great knowledge. It has fine-tuned my investing strategies... Your book is hard to set aside, as I read it all the time learning good techniques and analysis of stocks, ETF... Since I purchased your book in March, I have underlined, highlighted and placed tabs on top of pages for quick reference." - Aileron on this book.

"Great stuff, Tony. It's great to meet experienced traders such as yourself. I had a browse through the book and think your method is a little more refined than mine."
"Your strategy is very rules based and solid. I sometimes envy people who have developed something like this."

Making 50% in one month

I claim to have the best one-month performance ever for recommending 8 or more stocks without using options and leverage. My following return is 57% in a month or 621% annualized. They are slightly different as I calculated the average from the averages of three different accounts. The average buy date is 12/26/18 and the "current date" is 01/28/19.

The performance may not be repeated. I will use the same screen for the coming years and even the expected 10% (or 120% annualized) is very good.

I used the same screen for searching stock candidates. I spent a total of about 20 hours from Dec. 15, 2018 to Jan. 5, 2019.

Stock	Buy Price	Sold or Current Price	Buy date	Sold or Current date	Profit %	Profit % Ann.	Status
CHK	2.13	2.99	01/03/09	01/18/19	40%	982%	Sold
MNK	16.41	21.45	01/03/19	01/25/19	31%	510%	Sold
MNK	16.43	21.45	01/03/19	01/25/19	31%	507%	Sold
NNBR	5.68	8.58	12/26/18	01/28/19	51%	565%	
NNBR	5.72	8.58	12/26/18	01/28/19	66%	727%	
ESTE	4.35	6.45	12/26/18	01/18/19	48%	766%	Sold
LCI	4.61	8.29	12/21/18	01/28/19	80%	767%	
MDR	8.01	9.13	01/08/19	01/28/19	14%	255%	
YRCW	3.29	5.78	12/21/18	01/28/19	76%	727%	
YRCW	3.26	5.78	12/21/18	01/28/19	77%	742%	
ASRT	3.56	4.18	12/26/18	01/28/19	17%	193%	
UTCC	7.13	11.00	12/26/18	01/28/19	54%	600%	

YRCW	2.92	5.78	12/26/18	01/28/19	98%	1083%	

Best one-year return

I claim to have the best-performed article in Seeking Alpha history, an investing site, for recommending 15 or more stocks in one year after the publish date without using options and leverage.

https://seekingalpha.com/article/1095671-amazing-returns-velti-alcatel-lucent-alpha-natural-resources

Your choice for your next book

I was surprised that one told me $25 is a lot for an investing book. It could be less than a taxi cab to the airport attending a seminar, and the time is peanut comparatively.

"Art of investing 2nd Edition" should be your first choice. If you are short-term trading, I recommend "Sector Rotation: 21 Strategies" and "Shorting Stocks /ETFs 2nd Edition". These books together with "Using Fidelity" and "Using Finviz" share many articles.

A new book every Dec. 15 with a July update (not a promise) is my selections on stocks. So far, the returns of the selected stocks are phenomenal. "A nuclear war with China?" is my views on politics.

Appendix 3 - Our window to the investing world

The paperback version of this chapter can be found in the following link.
http://ebmyth.blogspot.com/2013/11/web-sites.html

- **General**
  Wikipedia / Investopedia /Yahoo!Finance / MarketWatch / Cnnfn / Morningstar /CNBC / Bloomberg / WSJ / Barron's / Motley Fool / TheStreet
- **Evaluate stocks**
  Finviz / SeekingAlpha / MSN Money / Zacks / Daily Finance / ADR / Fidelity / Earnings Impact / OpenInsider / NYSE /

NASDAQ / SEC / SEC for 10K and 10Q (quarterly) reports required to file for listed stocks in major exchanges.

- **Charts**
  BigCharts / FreeStockCharts / StockCharts /
- **Screens**
  Yahoo!Finance / Finviz / CNBC / Morningstar /
- **Besides stocks**
  123Jump / Hoover's Online / FINRA Bond Market Data / REIT /
  Commodity Futures / Option Industry
- **Vendors**
  AAII / Zacks / IBD / GuruFocus / VectorVest /
  Fidelity / Interactive Brokers / Merrill Lynch /
- **Economy.**
  Econday / EcoconStats / Federal Reserve / Economist /
- **Misc.**
  Dow Jones Indices / Russell / Wilshire /
  IRS / Wikinvest / ETF Database / ETF Trends /
  Nolo (estate planning) / AARP /

Appendix 4 - ETFs / Mutual Funds

What is an ETF
ETFs have basic differences from mutual funds: 1. Lower management expenses, 2. Trade ETFs same as stocks, and 3. Usually more diversified but not more selective than the related mutual funds such as NOBL vs FRDPX.

The major classifications of ETFs are 1. Simulating an index such as SPY, QQQ and DIA, 2. Simulating a sector such as XLE and SOXX, 3. Simulating an asset class such as GLD and SLV, 4. Simulating a country or a group of countries such as EWC and FXI, 5. Managed by a manager(s) such as ARKK, 6. Betting a market or sector to go down such as SH and PSQ, and 7. Leveraged (not recommended for beginners).

Fidelity: Index ETFs (https://www.fidelity.com/etfs/overview).
Wikipedia on ETF (http://en.wikipedia.org/wiki/Exchange-traded_fund).

List of ETFs
ETF database (Recommended): http://etfdb.com/
ETF Bloomberg: http://www.bloomberg.com/markets/etfs/
ETF Trends: http://www.etftrends.com/
A list of ETFs. Seeking Alpha.
http://etf.stock-encyclopedia.com/category/)
A list of contra ETFs (or bear ETFs)
http://www.tradermike.net/inverse-short-etfs-bearish-etf-funds/
Misc.: ETFGuide, ETFReplay
Fidelity low-cost index funds:
https://www.youtube.com/watch?v=zpKi4_IJvlY
Fidelity Annuity funds with performance data.
http://fundresearch.fidelity.com/annuities/category-performance-annual-total-returns-quarterly/FPRAI?refann=005

Other resources
Most subscription services offer research on ETFs. IBD has a strategy dedicated to ETFs and so does AAII to name a couple.

Seeking Alpha has extensive resources for ETF including an ETF screener and investing ideas. So is ETFdb.

Not all ETFs are created equal

Check their performances and their expenses.

When to use or not to use ETFs

I prefer sector mutual funds in some industries, as they have many bad stocks such as drug industry, banks, miners and insurers. Most mutual funds cannot time the market.

When you believe a sector is heading up (or contra ETF for heading down), but you do not have time to do research on specific stocks, buy an ETF for the sector; it is same for the market.

Half ETF
Taking out half of the stocks that score below the average in an index ETF could beat the same full ETF itself. I call it HETF (half the ETF). You heard it here first. To illustrate, sort the expected P/E (not including stocks with negative earnings) in ascending order and only include the stocks on the first half. Add more fundamental metrics. It will take a few minutes.

Disadvantages of ETFs
- When you have two stocks in a sector ETF one good one and one bad one, the ETF treats them the same. Stock pickers would buy the one that has a better appreciation potential.
- Sometimes the return could be misleading due to stock rotation. To illustrate this, on August 29, 2012, SHLD was replaced by LYB in a sector fund. SHLD was down by 4% and LYB was up by 4% primarily due to the switch. Unless you sell and buy at the right time (which is impossible), your return would not match the ETF's returns due to the replacement.
- Ensure the performance matches the corresponding index; it is hard due to excluding dividends.

Advantages of ETFs
- We have demonstrated that you can beat the market by using market timing. Between 2000 and Nov., 2013, you only exit and reenter the market 3 times and the result is astonishing.

- It is easy to rotate a sector vs. buying/selling all of the stocks in this sector. Rotating a sector is the same as trading a stock.
- The risk is spread out, and your portfolio is diversified especially for a market ETF or buying three or more ETFs in different sectors.
- Periodically the bad stocks in most funds are replaced by better stocks.
- Eliminate the time in researching stocks.

Leveraged ETFs

I do not recommend them. Some are 2x, 3x and even higher. They're too risky for beginners. However, when you are very sure or your tested strategy has very low drawdown, you may want to use them to improve performance. Most leveraged ETFs and contra ETFs have higher fees.

My basic ETF tables

I include some contra ETFs, mutual funds and Fidelity's annuity. Some of these may be interesting to you.

ETFs and funds come and go. Some ideas and classifications are my own interpretation. Refer to ETFdb for updated information. Not responsible for any error. Check out the ETF or fund before you take any action.

Table by market cap:

Category	ETF	Mutual Funds	Fidelity's Annuity	Contra ETF	Alternate
Size:					
Large Cap	DIA	See Blend		DOG	
	SPY			SH	FXAIX VOO
	QQQ			PSQ	FNCMX
	RYH				
Blend	IWD	BEQGX			
Growth	SPYG	FBGRX			FSPGX
Value	SPYV	DOGGX			FLCOX
Dividend	NOBL	FRDPX			

	VYM					
Mid Cap				FNBSC	MYY	
Blend	MDY	VSEQX				
Growth		STDIX				
		BPTRX				
Value		FSMVX				
Small Cap				FPRGC	SBB	FSSNX
Blend	IWM	HDPSX				
Growth		PRDSX				FECGX
Value		SKSEX				FISVX
Micro	IWC					
Multi						
Blend		VDEOX				
Growth		VHCOX				
Value		TCLCX				
Total						FSKAX
Bond						
Long Term (20)	VLV	BTTTX			TBF	
Mid Term (7 – 10)	VCIT	FSTGX				
Short Term (1 – 3 yrs.)	VCSH	THOPX				
Total	BOND	PONDX				
Corp Invest Grade	VCIT	NTHEX				
High Yield (junk)	PHB	SPHIX				
Muni	MUB	Check state				
Special situation						
Buy back	PKW					

Table by sectors:

Sector	ETF	Mutual Funds	Fidelity's Annuity
Banking[1]		FSRBK	
Regional	IAT		
Bio Tech	IBB	FBIOX	
	XBI	Large	
Consumer Dis.	XLY	FSCPX	FVHAC
Consumer Staple	XLP	FDFAX	FCSAC
Finance	KIE	FIDSX	FONNC
	IYF		
Energy	XLE	FSENX	FJLLC
Energy Service		FSESX	
Gold	GLD	FSAGX	
Gold Miner	GDX	VGPMX	
Health Care	IYH	FSPHX	FPDRC
	VHT	VGHCX	
House Builder	ITB	FSHOX	
	ITB	Perform	
Industrial	IYJ	FCYIX	FBALC
Material	VAW	FSDPX	
	IYM		
Oil	USO		
Oil Service	OIH	FSESX	
Oil Exploration	XOP		
Real Estate	VNQ	FRIFX	FFWLC
REIT	VNQ		
Retail	RTH	FSRPX	
	XRT		
Regional bank	KRE	FSRBX	
Semi Conduct	SMH		
Software	XSW	FSCSX	
	IGV		
Technology	XLK	FSPTX	FYENC
	FDN	FBSOX	
		ROGSX	
Telecomm.	VOX	FSTCX	FVTAC
Transport	XTN		

Page 217

	IYT		
Utilities	XLU	FSUTX	FKMSC
Wireless		FWRLX	

Footnote. [1] Also check Finance.

Table by countries outside the USA:

Country	ETF	Mutual Funds	Fidelity's Annuity	Alternate
Australia	EWA			
Brazil	EWZ			
Canada	EWC	FICDX		
China	FXI	FHKCX		
EAFE	EFA			
Emerging	VWO	FEMEX	FEMAC	FPADX
Europe	VGK	FIEUX		
Global	KXI	PGVFX		
Greece	GREK			
India	INDY	MINDX		
Indonesia	EIDO			
Latin America	ILF	FLATX		
Nordic		FNORX		
Hong Kong	EWH			
Japan	EWJ	FJPNX		
S. Africa	EZA			
S. Korea	EWY	MAKOX		
Singapore	EWS			
Taiwan	EWT			
	TUR			
United Kingdom	EWU			
Foreign:				
Combination				
Intern. Div.	IDV			FTIHX
Small Cap	SCZ			
Value	EFV			
Europe	VGK			

#Filler: Honey, my book can play music.
https://www.youtube.com/watch?v=HxGT5z6d-GA&list=PLMZa6mP7jZ2b1otqG4tfbgZpLEdh6YiNF

It may cut down commercials by casting it to TV.

Quick analysis of ETFs

Evaluate an ETF

ETFs are a basket of stocks according to the market, a specific sector, country or a specific theme.

Yahoo!Finance used to give the P/E of an ETF. Try to get it from ETFdb.com. Enter the symbol of the ETF such as XLU, and then select Valuation. If it is below 15 and above zero, it could be a value ETF. Also, if the current price is lower than its NAV, it is sold at a discount (or premium vice versa). Compare its YTD Return to SPY's.

Alternatively, get similar info from http://www.multpl.com/. In addition, this website provides the following metrics: Shiller P/E, Price/Sales, and Price/Book.

From Finviz.com, enter the ETF symbol. If SMA-20%, SMA-50% and SMA-200% are all positive, most likely the ETF is in an uptrend. To illustrate, SMA-200 is Simple Moving Average for the last 200 trading sessions (no trading on weekends and specific holidays). The percent is how much the stock price of the ETF is above the SMA. If the percent is negative, it means the stock price is below the SMA.

If your average holding period of your stocks is about 50 days, SMA-50% is more appropriate to you.

If RSI(14) > 65, it is probably oversold; if it is < 30, it is probably under-sold (indicating value).

In addition, ensure the ETF's average volume is high (I suggest more than 10,000 shares), the market cap is more than 300 M, and it has low fees. Most popular ETFs have these characteristics. Beginners should avoid leveraged ETFs.

How to determine if the sector has been recovered

It is easier to profit by following the uptrend of an ETF using the above info. It is hard to detect when the bottom of an ETF has been reached. If SMA-20%, SMA-50% and SMA-200% are all positive, most likely the ETF is in an uptrend or it has recovered. It does not always happen as predicted, so use stops to protect your investment.

An example

First, determine whether the market is risky. Most beginners should not invest in a risky market. Advanced investors can bet against the market or a specific sector by buying contra ETFs or puts.

Next, you want to limit the number of sector ETFs by selecting those that are either in an uptrend or hitting bottom (bottom is hard to predict). Personally I prefer sectors with long-term uptrends (indicated by articles found in many websites including cnnfn.com and Seeking Alpha.

For illustration purposes only for deteriorating market conditions, I would select the following ETFs: SPY (simulating the market based on large companies) and XLP (consumer staples). XLP should perform better than XLY (consumer discretionary) during a recession as those products are the necessities.

Technical indicators such as SMA-50 (Simple Moving Average for the last 50 sessions), SMA-200 and RSI(14) are obtained from Finviz.com and the rest are obtained from Yahoo!Finance.com. After you buy the ETF, use a stop loss to protect your investment. For example, bio tech sector moved up for many months until it crashed in 2015. Change the stop loss value every month to protect your gains in this case.

As of 2/5/2016	SPY	XLP (staples)	XLY (discret.)
Price	190	50	71
NAV	192	50	73
• Technical			
SMA-50	-4%	0%	-7%
SMA-200	-6%	2%	-7%
RSI(14)	44	50	36
Other	Double bottom at $186		
• Fundamental			
P/E	17	20	19
Yield	2.1%	2.5%	1.5%
YTD return	-5%	0.5%	-5%
Net asset	174 B	9 B	10 B

Explanation
• The figures may not be identical among websites due to the dates they are using.

- XLY has best discount among the 3 ETFs as most investors believe a recession is coming.
- XLP has less down trend among the 3 ETFs as expected.
- XLY is more undersold among the three as expected.
- Double bottom is a technical pattern that indicates the stock would surge upward.
- SPY has a better value according to its P/E.
- XLY's dividend is the least among the three as they have more tech companies in the ETF. They have to plow back the profits to research and development.
- XLP has the best YTD return among the three.
- As long as the asset is above 500 M (200 M for specialized ETFs), it is fine and all three pass this mark.

There are many metrics such as Debt/Equity not readily available from most websites. Many sites list the top holdings of a specific ETF. Just average the metrics of the top ten or so of its stock holdings.

www.ingramcontent.com/pod-product-compliance
Lightning Source LLC
Chambersburg PA
CBHW071256220526
45468CB00001B/160